Entrepreneurial Essentials:

UNCONVENTIONAL BUSINESS WISDOM AND BOLD TACTICS

by James D. Roumeliotis

Copyright © 2012 by James D. Roumeliotis
First Edition — August 2012

Cover concept: Vagelis Tasopoulos
Art direction: Elsa Sturm

ISBN
978-1-77097-611-5 (Hardcover)
978-1-77097-612-2 (Paperback)
978-1-77097-613-9 (eBook)

All rights reserved.

No part of this publication may be reproduced in any form, or by any means, electronic or mechanical, including photocopying, recording, or any information browsing, storage, or retrieval system, without permission in writing from the publisher.

Published by:

FriesenPress
Suite 300 — 852 Fort Street
Victoria, BC, Canada V8W 1H8

www.friesenpress.com

Distributed to the trade by The Ingram Book Company

Table of Contents

Preamble

Chapter I: Business Effectiveness

The 7 Key Principles for Business Success —
A Personal Belief Through Years of Practical Experience 1

The Inept Organization: Weak Leadership as the Culprit. 4

Innovative yet Effective Hiring Practices:
Unconventional HR Builds Benefits 10

Chapter II: Executive Leadership

Optimizing the Decision Making Process: Executive Leadership 16

The Anathema of Bureaucracy:
Dealing with its Fate and Embracing its Inverse 20

Chapter III: Sales Management Strategies

Plotting Sales Structure Strategy 24

Sales Force Dynamics: Instituting an Ideal Compensation Plan 30

Management by Tactics: A Sales Management Supervisory
Technique and its Effects on Sales Performance. 36

Sales Management: Focusing On Core Competencies for
Extraordinary Results. 40

Chapter IV: Marketing and Branding Tactics

Branding Strategies for a Fundamental Differentiation 49

Professional Branding Up Close and Personal:
Advice for the Private Practice 53

ME, Inc.: The Impact of Personal Branding in Strategic Marketing . . . 59

Exploiting the Benefits of Niche Marketing: Strategic Marketing 64

Demonstrate Rather than Tell: How Experiential Marketing is
Creating a Sea-Change in the World of Branding and Advertising . . . 69

Ambiance Marketing: A Multi-Sensory Approach
to Attracting and Retaining Clientele 74

Marketing Strategy vs. Public Relations — In Tune with The Times . . 79

Lifestyle Branding: Engagement and Total Experience 84

Branding Bottled Water:
Differentiating a Commodity Through Various Tactics. 89

Post Recession Marketing Approach:
Adapting the Message to a Changing Consumer 96

Chapter V: Customer Engagement

The Customer Experience: Building a Customer-Centric Organization 99

A Philosophy Named CUSTOMER SERVICE —
How to Refine it and Maintain It 105

Chapter VI: Design and Innovation

The Essence of Creative Consumer Product and Packaging Design 112

Chapter VII: The Luxury Domain

Defining the Luxury Brand. 117

Luxury Condominium Project Marketing:
Challenging Conventional Wisdom is Heads-Up Branding 124

Upscale Restaurant Marketing with an Attitude —
Seducing & Retaining Discerning Patrons through
Lean and Challenging Times. 127

Embracing a New Paradigm Shift in the
Luxury Product Domain — Post Recession 132

Business Outside of the Corporation

How to Run an Effective Political Campaign —
a Synopsis for the Aspiring Candidate. 136

BIBLIOGRAPHY 141

I dedicate this book to my twin daughters, Athena and Suzana-Maria who are my purpose in life — as well as to all like-minded business people and professionals the world-over.

"An empowered organization is one in which individuals have the knowledge, skill, desire, and opportunity to personally succeed in a way that leads to collective organizational success."

— Stephen R. Covey

Preamble

Although I have been a prolific writer for many years, this book is my initial release — the content of which I was eager to share with those who are willing to approach business practices from a different perspective. This is not a typical "how to" book although there is plenty of "how to" in it. The subject matter herein includes an updated collection of my published and well received articles.

This project was a personal lifetime goal which I was keen to achieve prior to my midlife. The idea and inspiration for this book came from more than 30 years as a practitioner in the areas of business development (B2B and B2C), sales management, customer engagement, marketing/branding (online/offline most notably the luxury sector), public relations, project management and entrepreneurship — all in diverse fields involving products, as well as services and spanning three countries and beyond. Along with my practical experience and having dealt with adverse circumstances locally and overseas, I have also learned by paying particular attention to mistakes/failures and successes made by individuals in key leadership positions. In addition, over the years I have become a student of each business/industry I have been involved with through continuous and relentless training, research and occasional academic work. You will not find much empirical evidence in here as the book was not intended for academia. However, I do encourage any professional to apply the ideas which, if executed capably, should yield the results which worked for me and many others. There are, plenty of suggestions with common sense adaptable possibilities for any flexible contemporary organization.

As a resourceful, knowledgeable and caring person, I very much enjoy offering both solicited and unsolicited advice, along with a dose of motivation, particularly to those who genuinely care to help themselves. This time I am delighted to give back to various business professionals (salespeople, sales managers, company/divisional heads, marketers to name a few) thoughts and ideas that they can apply in their relevant fields of endeavor. The ideas are equally applicable in the public sector.

Moreover, having been involved in a couple of municipal/political campaigns as a manager/adviser, I decided to include some helpful advice on managing an effective political campaign.

Every subject in this book, regardless of its scope of business, has a similar theme: it involves loyal, dedicated and well-trained people who are empowered to think "outside the box" (lateral thinking) and apply their creative ideas usually with stellar results.

I have produced seven chapters in distinct categories to make the book simple to follow and a practical way to search for a specific subject of interest.

Chapter I: Business Effectiveness — *Subject matter which covers the degree to which objectives are achieved and the extent to which targeted problems are solved. In contrast to efficiency, effectiveness is determined without reference to costs and, whereas efficiency means "doing the thing right," effectiveness means "doing the right thing".*

Chapter II: Executive Leadership — *When you are in any position of leadership, it is no longer about you — it is all about the people following your lead. The topics in this chapter describe what it takes to lead including suggestions for practical and effective decision making and ways to eliminate the stifling bureaucracy.*

Chapter III: Sales Management Strategies — *Creating a successful sales strategy will allow sales managers and their sales team to focus on the right customers. Here all aspects of sales management are covered including hiring the right candidates, training/development, tactics and compensation.*

Chapter IV: Marketing and Branding Tactics — *Well targeted and strategic marketing engages your audience as it makes a connection with them. Several elements of marketing, including focused marketing and branding strategy, are covered in this section. They work together to reinforce and strengthen the brand image.*

Chapter V: Customer Engagement — *Repeated interactions a client experiences with a company are considered touch points. Topics here include customer service, as well as how the experience a customer interaction or encounter that can influence the customer's perception of a product, service, or brand.*

Chapter VI: Design and Innovation — *As design is an important element of innovation that is often overlooked, this section describes how we interact with and experience products which in turn, will determine which ones consumers will appreciate for both their beauty and functionality and therefore purchase.*

Chapter VII: The Luxury Domain — *This specific and higher-priced tier of offer in almost any product or service category has its own rules for success. This chapter puts into perspective lifestyle, customer aspirations, types of wealth, and high-end trends along with branding.*

Amongst the people I would like to thank for their collaboration with my writing project are: Thomas C. Mylonas <www.dotkite.eu>, who co-authored with me, "*The Essence of Creative Consumer Product and Packaging Design*", **Andrew Scharf** <www.whitefieldconsulting.com> for his valuable input, including **FirstEditing.com** for their professional editorial work and content flow enhancement.

I encourage dialogue regarding any of the enclosed subject matter. Comments/views can be communicated to me at jdr@affluencemarketing.ca

I am available for individual coaching and consulting, as well as for group presentations and speaking engagements on any of the topics in this book. My seminars are known to be concise and quite visually focused. Most of my slides contain one or two lines of text and an image. Watching my presentation makes you feel like you are watching a documentary — yet all of my presentations can be custom tailored to a specific audience.

James D. Roumeliotis
June 2012

"No institution can possibly survive if it needs geniuses or supermen to manage it. It must be organized in such a way as to be able to get along under a leadership composed of average human beings."

— Peter Drucker

"Business, more than any other occupation, is a continual dealing with the future; it is a continual calculation, an instinctive exercise in foresight."

— Henry R. Luce

Entrepreneurial Essentials *is what everybody needs to have if they want to be successful entrepreneurs. In today's education-inflated society, James shows how developing your entrepreneurial skills are paramount in building a successful business. With a record high numbers of MBA and PhD's the next frontier in business will be creative thinking to blaze new trails in the business world. Unconventional Business Wisdom is not taught, it is experienced! Let James Roumeliotis guide you through your journey in business!*

Baastian van Gent
Vice Chairman, Europe China Foundation

If you want to grasp key ideas on business tactics, and to understand how successful processes can be achieved thanks to clear and numerous examples, then Entrepreneurial Essentials *will surely be a very useful tool. Its approach is pragmatic, and also includes a sharp analysis of the sometimes hermetic luxury brand industry.*

Stéphane Dellile
Managing Director & CEO at Chopard, Japan

As a medical practitioner, I found James Roumeliotis's marketing and branding contents very relevant, as well as achievable to implement into my own practice for success.

Dr. Lila Bratani
Plastic and Aesthetic Surgeon, Stuttgart, Germany

Entrepreneurial Essentials, *combines research with proven practices in actual situations. The book offers a combination of books smarts and street smarts with sound advice in the most essential areas of business.*

Leslie Powell
Business Consultant (for Franchisees) at
McDonald's Restaurants of Canada Ltd.

continued...

You have covered an amazingly extensive array of topics in an easy to understand and to appreciate style. I am keen to share your wisdom and insights on 'branding and customer engagement' with my associates. Your book should be reviewed and discussed by the 2nd year MBA student-executives.

Bhaskar Patel
General Manager at Cybersoft Technologies Inc.

The author has a knack for providing succinct, practical and well organized advice on a vast range of topics. The chapter on political campaigns should be read at the outset by all who are considering running for public office.

Wade Staddon, BA, MUP
Councillor - District 3, Chair - BEAC; City
of Beaconsfield, Quebec, Canada

Chapter I: Business Effectiveness

The 7 Key Principles for Business Success —
A Personal Belief Through Years of
Practical Experience

1) VIABLE PRODUCT OR SERVICE WITH A PASSIONATE PERSON BEHIND IT

It should fulfill a need, offer a benefit, be innovative and differentiate itself. It's also imperative that the entrepreneur is passionate about the product/service, empowers his/her staff, as well as practices/conveys business ethics. To excel in the business, the entrepreneur must have the right mindset and attitude. This includes drive, perseverance, tenacity, and an undying belief in himself/herself and the value he/she adds. He/She must also be willing to embrace the concept that he/she takes complete ownership for his/her results. He/She can't blame the marketplace, the economy or the employees for failure. In the end, it's the entrepreneur making the decisions.

2) CAPITAL

Critical and can vary depending on the size of the undertaking. Start your capital search with a good business plan that shows investors and lenders your company's potential. Furthermore, take advantage of any government loan program created for start-ups.

Expect to realistically invest about 30% of your own money based on the total value of the project. Last but not least, cash-flow is the lifeblood of your business if you're going to sustain the operation financially.

3) MARKETING & SALES

Advertise, publicize, be first, different, daring and memorable. Deliver on those promises and constantly remain customer focused.

Sales, on the other hand, are part of the marketing function. They include business development and account management. Sales are crucial to business because they are the bottom line, whereas marketing is about getting a product known. However, at the end of the day, it's about the need for a constant stream of new business which brings in the necessary cash flow.

4) PEOPLE

Don't simply HIRE well-educated and experienced people. It's most important to hire MOTIVATED, dedicated, coachable staff with interpersonal skills. Moreover, make certain that the people you hire fit-in with your corporate culture. Your organization should also foster an atmosphere of innovation and creativity through leadership. Work for staff should be meaningful rather than a chore. These conditions can't help but breed success. Implement an orientation workshop for new recruits and an occasional training program. Invest in your key employees!

5) SYSTEMS — STRUCTURE

Consider publishing an "Operations Manual" and continuously enforce its procedures. Without a structure, the chances of failure increases. Everyone should be on the same page and embrace best practices for quality results with consistency.

6) STRICT INTERNAL FINANCIAL CONTROLS & CASH FLOW

Watch them closely, borrow wisely and don't overspend. Watch your financial ratios and yields (where applicable). The success of your business is, in many ways, measured by the bottom line. Even if you hired a full-time accountant, you would still need to have a fundamental knowledge of accounting, how it works, and how to apply its basic principles in order to run a flourishing business.

7) CONTINUOUS IMPROVEMENT, INNOVATION AND SUSTAINED GROWTH

This is by no means a one-time event but rather an on-going process.

"If you don't drive your business, you will be driven out of business."

- B. C. Forbes

The Inept Organization: Weak Leadership as the Culprit

How often do you come across a company, either as a consumer or at a business relationship level, and realize how frustrating it is to deal with?

To understand and penetrate the corporate governing structure and "culture", you need look no further than the upper echelon of the hierarchical tree. It is here that procedural decisions are shaped and executed. An entity's leadership is expected to head the enterprise by governing its long-term growth and sustained wealth.

Moreover, there is a constant search for the "right" human resources. Recruited and fresh talent must resemble the leadership in tone and style. Call it the organization's DNA. Exceptional organizations are good at these types of corporate strategies, thus strengthening performance effectively.

I have noticed that in certain types of B2B transactions, there can be scope for unscrupulous behavior. One or both parties are tempted by "disservice" during their business exchange. Shortsightedness might lend itself to make this underhanded approach appear "profitable" on paper. Such relationships inevitably end badly because they are not conceived with trust or respect.

SUCCESS BREEDS SUCCESS

Companies that foster the right attitudes and strategies put the firm on track for success. Examining their corporate histories, you can witness a trajectory of growth. They have a tendency to dominate their markets and "win" through competent talent, innovation, and an entrepreneurial mindset within the leadership at the executive level. These choices underscore the prosperity and rapid growth of the institution. An examination of Google or Facebook shows this quite nicely. They are not built like "traditional" corporations nor do they act like them.

Organizational leadership is accountable for creating value for customers, employees and its owners/investors. When Bill Gates conceived Microsoft, he put the firm on track for providing constituent audiences with what nobody else could provide. Understanding "asset" management in an expanded meaning of the term guaranteed that Microsoft would succeed under Gates stewardship.

The opposite is equally true. When top executives lack knowledge or experience for board positions, they should not be promoted to these leadership roles. Some family-owned firms run afoul here and this brings up the issues of sustainability and corporate governance. Another weakness in running an organization, in my view, is pushing for short-term profitability at the expense of solid planning. For example, with large organizations, competence is not the primary value but rather connections, politics, and clever tactics. Such "benefits" can usually compensate for incompetence.

No firm can continue to prosper unless it attracts fresh and eager talent. Despite the dilemmas within the financial world, top organizations consistently lure new talent with lucrative compensation packages. It is easier for a firm such as Goldman to tap the "best" because of its reputation, size and success than a small local financial player.

When Goldman recruits they know where to look, whether it is Harvard or the London Business School. Prospects will already contain the seeds of the corporate culture in their past. Given the "right" conditions, new talent blossoms. Qualifications are never enough. They are a starting point reinforced by attitude and values. The selection and screening process is designed by HR to weed out inappropriate candidates.

Take the case of Michael Page, the global recruitment firm. Ever wonder when you pass one of their buildings on a Friday evening why the staff at the pub all seem to resemble one another, whether men or women? They were intentionally selected to match a model.

To give you another example, Microsoft's interview process includes quizzing candidates with challenging technical questions. This practice not only assesses problem-solving and knowledge ability, but also explores the ability to perform under pressure, which is a key skill required to succeed in Microsoft's intense work environment.

One thing is dead certain. The best-managed companies have "one" factor in common:

They are constant achievers in their respective industries. These companies exude managerial excellence. Financial performance is the result of this style of management. Take the case of the Westinghouse Air Brake Company, a 19th-century business that still thrives because it is one of the companies with the "best management" in the USA.

DEEDS NOT SLOGANS

Companies with inept leadership usually fail in the first year or two, but even established companies can stumble badly when they outgrow the capabilities of the founding team. Research by the U.S. Bureau of Labor Statistics demonstrates that nearly 6/10 businesses shut down within the first 4 years of operation.

To be a successful entrepreneur is not an effortless task. It takes plenty of sacrifice. A new generation of young entrepreneurs think the road is smooth and a fast track to easy wealth. Not everyone will become Mark Zuckerberg. Obstacles and sacrifice are part of the deal. Harnessing opportunity and overcoming challenges on a daily basis to top the competition is constant work. These conditions are true no matter what the sector of business engagement or company size.

Telltale signs of weak organizations can be traced to inept leadership. The following points highlight the deficiencies:

- Poor customer service — slow or no customer inquiry replies — abysmal handling of sales and service complaints. Service is portrayed as a reward, not a right or benefit.

- No Unique Selling/Value Proposition. Companies need to define and articulate their unique value proposition and deliver on it consistently. Create the platform for sustainable and competitive advantage.

- Operational deficiencies — various ailments and no structure

- Absence of or very little communication amongst staff and management. Divisions aren't well-coordinated and do not function as a team.

- No transparency. There is hardly any openness from management.

- Unethical practices — short-term selfish objectives in search of market share. Top executives should promote social norms and principles as moral agents.

- Lack of proper execution of decisions and with new products/services.

- Productivity incentives should be implemented to boost results and employee morale. People must be given a reason to work hard and be efficient.

- Creativity is practically non-existent. An absence of innovation and employee empowerment will hurt progress and stifle new ideas.

- No clear vision/strategy — there needs to be a strategic vision that reflects a truly unmet need and has the commitment of a dedicated CEO. That means that there is a well-defined target audience with a distinct value position that is differentiated, meaningful, and deliverable.

- A weak sales force along with an unattractive compensation plan.

- Favoring nepotism and bias — promoting family members over other qualified employees often leads to resentment or, worse, prompts valuable non-family employees to leave the company.

- Poor hiring practices — should hire for attitude and train for skills.

- Slow/delayed decision-making process — too many layers — overwhelming bureaucratic structure.

- High turnover, which leads to poor employee morale, reduced intellectual capital, lower service levels, higher operational costs and decreased productivity.

- Management in a state of denial about their organization's shortcomings — remaining with the dysfunctional status quo

- No channel strategy. Some companies focus on building a product, but don't think through how to get it into the hands of customers. Even if your product is great, unless you can sell directly, you may be dead in the water without strong channel partners.

- The hidden game — corporate politics — power plays by a handful of individuals for their own benefit to the detriment of their colleagues and the company.

- Misrepresentation of brand(s) – too much hype — empty promises — not delivering on expectations — leads to dissatisfied clients who will alienate the brand.

- Weak financial controls — cash flow dilemmas — over leveraged/undercapitalized (high debt-to-capital ratio) – not reinvesting a certain percentage of profits for future growth.

- Absence of sound marketing program(s) and/or brand strategy. A brand is defined by how it behaves, from the products it builds to how it treats its customers, to the suppliers with whom it works.

- Growing too fast and not staying on course as the company grows.

- Lack or very little employee training & development.

- Deficient in control systems — reactive rather than pro-active.

- Lack of continuous improvements or complacent.

Top executives need to be accountable to the ownership or Board of Directors — whichever applies, or at least to an outside arm's length and neutral party such as an adviser who can also play "devil's advocate" when necessary.

GOOD ORGANIZATIONS MATTER

The way to solve an organizational problem is to confront the structural issues with a moral sense of purpose and ethics.

For its clients to receive stellar service, the firm must have its house in order. Besides structure and an efficient operation, employees should be trained and empowered to do their jobs efficiently.

Seth Godin, a renowned marketing strategist, stated succinctly: "If you want to build a caring organization, you need to fill it with caring people and then get out of their way. When your organization punishes people for caring, don't be surprised when people stop caring. When you free your employees to act like people (as opposed to cogs in a profit-maximizing efficient machine) then the caring can't help but happen."

Companies that disrespect their employees and shut-out clients get willfully isolated and have a short life span through an erosion of market share and significant loss of revenue. A company's goal should place emphasis on serving its people properly and fairly. Higher morale generates higher profits — though occasionally other priorities hinder that objective, for example, self-serving behavior by certain executives.

Enterprises spanning a wide array of industries, have earned distinction as "well-" or "best-" managed" by demonstrating business excellence through a meticulous and independent process that evaluates their management abilities and practices — by focusing on innovation, continuous training, brainstorming and caring for their employees' well-being — as well as investing in meeting the needs of their clients.

Well-run companies thrive no matter what and learn from their mistakes.

"Hire people, who are better than you are, then leave them to get on with it. Look for people who will aim for the remarkable, who will not settle for the routine."

— David Ogilvy

Innovative yet Effective Hiring Practices: Unconventional HR Builds Benefits

There is a daily news organization that utilizes some of the most unconventional hiring practices. They appear more qualitative than most journalism establishments. Their hiring editors evaluate recruits based on "personality and approach" to the news. Previously, HR used ideals of value and merit.

Roughly translated, this means that today, the recruitment practices are lengthy and involved including interviews with editors and a 30-minute writing test for every position. The subject matter of the essay is open to the applicant. Reactions to such hiring procedures show character or lack of character — initiative or mediocrity. Someone with fortitude will undoubtedly shine-out under these conditions and work culture.

Average hiring procedures, however, hold sway in most organizations. Companies either rely on outdated interview techniques or convoluted exams. Some base their decision- making on "feeling." At best, this technique can result in high turnover. What it *does* show is that a company's hiring practices is indicative of their culture. HR and the manager needing the staff should conduct the HR process in tandem, with the same list of procedures, to ensure their objectives are correlated.

Unfortunately, due to time constraints, lack of interest or weak corporate culture, the HR procedures degenerate into a bureaucratic mess, which lacks inspiration or innovation. Identifying the right talent requires the creative and innovative culture drawn from top management. HR should not be seen as an "internal" outsourcer. To draw top talent an organization most show that they are also "top-drawer."

Although this is not always the case in practice, both candidate and company should be "reviewing" each other for a mutual collaboration of talent and objectives pursued within the organization in need of new personnel at any level.

Taken from a slightly different angle, HR and senior management should view recruitment as it views customers. Customers are "wooed" so that brand loyalty is instilled in the purchase decision. The same reflexes should be instilled in the recruitment area. Loyalty can only be won through a mutual commitment. Salary is only part of motivation. Incentives and purpose are the other vectors. Considering today's mobility in hiring and firing, talent is unafraid to move to another organization if they are dissatisfied. Talent recruitment and retention therefore requires a new and better-honed focus, which in my opinion is severely lacking in general.

Think of the example of Google. HR makes it quite clear what the corporate culture demands and expects. You cannot keep these people without going outside the box. Examining magazines such as "Entrepreneur" and other trendy business publications in the States introduces you to exciting new corporate cultures and mentalities that foster the more effective HR spirit. Whether you are the one joining a company or hiring, both parties see the act of "recruitment" as an investment.

Simply put: Is the investment worth it?

HR needs to take a lesson from men's tailoring at its finest and go bespoke. The assembly line mentality instituted by Henry Ford is obsolete.

HIRING LIKE IT SHOULD TO BE — UPDATING CURRENT PRACTICES

"Hire for attitude and train for skill" should be the HR mantra. Employment requires a new definition: The attraction and retention of top talent in line with HR and cost. To get such HR talent on board your corporate ship, you will have to rethink your own view on employment.

Do you want just employees in the old sense of the term? Or do you value the concept of "empowerment" or dare I say "ownership"?

In today's business vortex, everything needs to be channeled through the concepts of service and added value. Lip service is pointless. Even in the most technical jobs, skills are only part of the whole picture.

Take the example of Southwest Airlines as a working case study. The firm is rated by *Fortune Magazine* as one of the best places to work for in America, requires every pilot to have a 737 aircraft type rating before this person is considered for hire. This rating, given by the Federal Aviation Administration, essentially says a pilot is qualified to be the captain of a Boeing 737. It signifies that all first officers are qualified to fly as captains, although it will take about six years to achieve "captain" status.

Over at Zappos, CEO Tony Hsieh says his company hires in favor of personality over job experience every time. "One of our core values is to be humble. So if there is someone who is really talented, and we know they will make an immediate impact on our top or bottom line, but they are really egotistical, then we won't hire them," he explains.

In person, the front-line staffers at brick and mortar shops or offices should be well-groomed, well-spoken, patient and properly trained to delicately handle clients.

The Boston Consulting Group and McKinsey & Co., two prestigious management-consulting firms, require more than just good grades when hiring someone. They aspire to change clients, industries, business, even society. For this reason, their consultants' success depends on their talent more than their degree. People with a background in many subjects such as business, natural sciences, philosophy, finance, and engineering, history — thrive at those highly reputable firms. They do, however, seek certain common traits.

The decision maker or hiring manager — the one who is going to work, lead and empower the prospective employee/subordinate — should be the one that undertakes the second and subsequent interviews. This person is the one who will have to deal with and get along with the appointee.

Hiring a person is similar to "marriage." Before you commit to each other for the long run, time should be spent talking and working together in various real-life work environments and situations. That is a practical way to decide whether you belong together. In other words, the courting process should be substantive.

As a practical rule, the less predictable you make the interview format; the more likely you are to truly understand the candidate being interviewed.

Another constructive idea is for the hiring manager to ask candidates to perform any of the following:

1. Do a brief presentation on a pertinent subject matter

2. Review their company website and provide written recommendations for improvement prior to the initial interview

3. Participate in some relevant pre-employment training to see how well they learn and interact with others

4. For a sales-related position, meet with a sales manager who can determine their knowledge of their market

Ideally, as opposed to waiting for people to apply for vacant positions, successful companies spend more time continuously searching for high-caliber people, particularly from within their organization or via referrals/recommendations from their loyal employees.

EXAMINING PAST BEHAVIOR INDICATORS

The following tools and processes will help vet candidates efficiently, as well as produce higher-quality candidates who will fit into your organization, contribute to its success and remain there for the long haul.

- **Utilizing pre-employment tests:** Professionally developed and properly validated employment tests can help a company's hiring process by increasing the likelihood of recruiting candidates who will perform well on the job. This is more commonly used when hiring for a sales/business development related position.

In addition, pre-employment testing can help ensure alignment between the employee selection process and desired business outcomes such as lower staff turnover, increased sales, and higher customer satisfaction. Research* has shown that cognitive aptitude tests, for example, are much more accurate predictors of job performance than are other widely used employee selection techniques. For example, a comprehensive survey of peer-reviewed studies of the predictive validity of various selection techniques concluded that aptitude tests are twice as predictive as job interviews, three times as predictive as experience, and four times as predictive as education level.

Source: Heneman and Judge, Staffing Organizations, 4th ed and Criteria: Corp. – Pre-employment Testing: Whitepaper

- **Situational/Behavioral Interview Questions:** How do you screen for attitudes such as, flexibility, unselfishness, initiative, or a tendency to take risks?

    The idea is to ask a candidate to describe how they would handle a certain situation, or what they would do under certain circumstances. Begin by creating targeted questions to get at the specific attitudes you are seeking. For example, if you are looking to hire someone who shows a history of "doing whatever it takes" you could say, "*Tell me about a time when you bent the rules or went above and beyond the call of duty to meet a customer's need?*"

- **Case Study Scenario Interviews:** These are widespread at the top-consulting firms. During this stage of the interview process, candidates are asked to develop a recommendation for a fictitious client by analyzing the relevant facts and demonstrating their ability to formulate a supportable conclusion. Although there is no single correct answer, there are a limited number of sound, defensible conclusions.

    At the end of exercise, they will receive feedback that illustrates the kind of thinking the firm interviewers will be looking for. It normally takes a little less than an hour for each candidate to work his/her way through the assignment.

THE FINAL ANALYSIS

Although traditional hiring has focused primarily on evaluating a candidate's skills and technical qualifications, a competency-based approach includes an analysis of a candidate's behavioral characteristics as well. Emphasis should be placed on hiring someone who will more than fulfill the job's minimum requirements. Potential candidates ought to have the capability of making a positive impact on the bottom line, as well as have the potential for being promoted later. Hiring should be an ongoing process, where talent is brought in early to the organization and developed for future business prospects.

The way you treat potential candidates reflects your company's image. It forms part of the word-of-mouth advertising, and with social media at almost everyone's disposal, can help or harm a company's reputation. If anything, this person is or can be your B2C customer.

Shortsightedness does not yield long-term benefits. Thus, the hiring model/process you establish today will determine the kind of culture, service standards, and the kind of reputation you will have tomorrow. It also keeps turnover very low. From a hiring manager's point of view, it's important to get multiple looks at a candidate and to give a candidate multiple looks at your company — even if it takes a bit longer.

"Be willing to make decisions. That's the most important quality in a good leader. Don't fall victim to what I call the 'ready-aim-aim-aim-aim syndrome'. You must be willing to fire."

—T. Boone Pickens

Chapter II: Executive Leadership

Optimizing the Decision Making Process: Executive Leadership

Face it! Like it or not you are defined by the decisions you make. Think of successful organizations and the people responsible for guiding their authority and well-being. Often, high performance is the result of an executive choosing the right move at the right time. It's not purely a lucky streak. Corporate strategy is not "Black Jack" nor 5-card stud poker.

Decision-making is a complex activity and at times a long process. Your ability to identify and excel in your decision-making tasks will greatly increase the chances that the choices you make will have a strong and positive impact on your organization. Why take any additional risks when you know instinctively that this is the case to sound growth and prosperity?

HOW TO GET STARTED

Your first step is to understand the external and internal factors that affect decision-making, from aspects of the organizational environment to your personal decision-making preferences. While you aren't always able to control these influences, recognizing and identifying these factors will enable you to take them into consideration as you strive to achieve the best decision outcome.

REALITY CHECK

Every day you make sense of what goes on around you by interpreting what you see and hear, taking into account your past experiences, values, needs, attitudes, and goals. Even your understanding of what another person says is only an estimate, as you can never completely share the viewpoint of someone else concerning the world.

Given the increasing complexity of organizational life, along with the quantity of information that must be processed, it is no wonder executives too often experience stress as they strive to balance agendas and please many of their people.

It can happen that you put a lot of time and effort into a decision study or a formal analysis, only to be disappointed in the results. When this happens, you need to re-evaluate both the information that went into the analysis including your expectations.

On the one hand, no process is any better than the information that goes into it and when you get a result that your experience suggests may be flawed or biased, this is a strong indication to probe.

On the other hand, it's extremely tempting to tinker with the data until you receive a result that you're happier with — but this is a form of deception that can lead to an adverse outcome. In this case, it helps to remind yourself to maintain a high standard of accuracy and objectivity and to seek a reality check from someone whose judgment you respect and who's not personally involved in the decision.

The decisions you make are only as good as the process you use to make them. Asking yourself the following questions will help you to assess whether or not you are on the right track:

1. Have I done adequate research and gathered all of the appropriate information for the subject matter at hand?

2. Have I considered all of the stakeholders and their probable responses to various decision outcomes?

3. Have I been honest in assessing my own decision making style and taken that into account?

4. Have I recognized and acknowledged my personal agendas and bias?

5. Have I considered the various options available to me in selecting the most appropriate decision making method?

6. Have I solicited the advice and assistance that was required?

7. Am I prepared to be accountable for the consequences of the decisions I make?

You have the responsibility for making decisions that deeply affect your employees' performance, morale and your organization's future. You cannot afford to rely on personal preferences or hunches alone.

Now that you are familiar with some practical, yet highly effective approaches offered here, your challenge is to develop a positive future possible through the decisions that you make today.

BOTTOM LINE

Your decisions are only as good as the information you use to make them. The cliché "Garbage in, garbage out" applies here. Your ability to recognize bias and evaluate the reliability and validity of the information you gather can make a tremendous difference in the effectiveness of your decisions.

"You will never understand bureaucracies until you understand that for bureaucrats, procedure is everything and outcomes are nothing."

—Thomas Sowell

The Anathema of Bureaucracy: Dealing with its Fate and Embracing its Inverse

According to Wikipedia, the word "bureaucracy" is defined as "The collective organizational structure, procedures, protocols and set of regulations in place to manage activity, usually in large organizations and government." In other words, it's a frustrating, rigid, process-driven, and a snail-paced institution. This shouldn't exist in democratic countries and ought to be controlled by developing nations if they are to effortlessly succeed. Not doing so, bureaucracy will become increasingly self-serving, complacent and breed corruption, rather than properly serve society as its intention.

In the private sector, if people don't work productively, their businesses will go bankrupt. But, in the public sector, seniority trumps performance regardless of employee efficiency or lack thereof. Competence in an organization is directly linked with its organizational system. In bureaucracy the hierarchy is typically very complex with many levels providing a highly differentiated structure of authority.

The faceless bureaucracy also exists in the private sector. Employees there get frustrated when they can't perform their work in a wholesome way because of restrictive yet superfluous rules set by their organization. Add to that corporate politics and it's not hard to see why there are high levels of employee exodus/turnover due to their discontent. There are organizations which thrive on their ability to allow individuals to remain faceless. It permits them to act badly which is not in the best interest of their customers.

BUREAUCRACY IN ACTION — OR RATHER INACTION

When it comes to shipping packages, I despise doing so at the post office because every time I go, their employees look for a reason not to ship it. Either "Too much tape!" or "Not enough tape!". On the other hand, I really enjoy bringing my packages to Fedex or The UPS store. The folks there have a totally different approach as they're not looking for a reason to say no but rather for an opportunity to say yes. "Here's some tape, we'll just add it right here…" The obvious reason is that the person at the post office has no incentive to make a sale. He/she knows that whether I'm well-served or not this person will still collect his/her paycheck, benefits and keep their job, in all probability, until retirement age.

If a company or government institution is in the service domain, then its people should look for ways to say "yes" at every interaction, provided they are not doing anything illegal or losing substantial amounts of money for their employer.

EMBRACE CHANGE, NOT BE PARALYZED BY IT

Organizations with a large bureaucracy struggle to make fast decisions. Bureaucracy creates a climate in which the customer is not as important as the management and the company's other employees. It also kills the organization's competitive spirit. As Jack Welch, former CEO of the industrial powerhouse, GE, has stated, "Bureaucracy is the enemy — it means waste, slow decision making and unnecessary approvals." Welch felt that ridding the company of wasteful bureaucracy was everyone's job. He urged all his employees to fight it. "Disdaining bureaucracy" became an important part of GE's shared values, At Google, the role of the manager is that of an aggregator of viewpoints, not the dictator of decisions.

For an organization to avoid the complacency and bureaucratic trap, it should encourage creative thinking, consider making innovation its foundation, as well as cut-out layers of its bloated management structure for a leaner decision making process. Innovation is what a business should be putting into effect as often as it's required for its long-term existence. The term "innovation" is widely described as: "Leading to significant organizational improvements in relation to enhanced or new business products, services, or internal processes." This involves acting on creative ideas to make some specific and tangible difference in the domain in which the innovation occurs. The old adage that goes something along the lines of "If it isn't broken, don't fix it" is a paradigm which doesn't sit well today with forward-thinking companies that thrive on practical improvements. There's nothing wrong with change if done to enhance or replace the status quo. It's part of collective progress. For this to work everyone, from the top brass down to the low labor employee, must embrace continuous change, rather than resist it. That may be more easily said than done due to typical resistance emerging from people due to fear of the unknown. It should be up to management to persuade their subordinates of the mutual benefits of change.

The following are **five recommendations** for managing creative employees.

1. **Accommodate:** Have an open door policy and offer an element of flexibility with employee schedules;

2. **Stimulate:** Encourage creative thinking not simply with words but also with rewards;

3. **Recognize:** Reward with greater autonomy and praise in front of peers;

4. **Direct lightly:** Avoid micromanaging and offer feedback;

5. **Progressive environment:** Avert unnecessarily restrictive rules and bureaucracy within the organization.

ADHOCRACY AS THE ACCEPTED WISDOM FOR ORGANIZATIONS TO FLOURISH

Author and expert on management issues, Robert H. Waterman, Jr., defines adhocracy as "any form of organization that cuts across normal bureaucratic lines to capture opportunities, solve problems, and get results." For Henry Mintzberg, a management guru, an adhocracy is a complex and dynamic organizational form. It is different from bureaucracy and considers bureaucracy a thing of the past, and adhocracy one of the future since it's very good at problem-solving and innovations and thrives in a changing environment.

That said, a company that works under a bureaucracy is very structured in its rules and hierarchy with mediocrity prevailing. Everyone knows their specific role, they specialize in that role, and know nothing, or very little, about the roles of their co-workers. On the other hand, a company that functions as an adhocracy experiences an organic structure where hierarchy barely exists. As a result, all members of such an organization have the authority to make decisions and to take actions affecting its future.

"Remember that it is not where you come from, or not even where you are; it is where you are going that matters most."

— Bo Bennett

Chapter III: Sales Management Strategies

Plotting Sales Structure Strategy

Structuring your sales organization has an enormous impact. This key and elemental issue in marketing poses several key questions for any marketing strategist. Let's start with some of the elemental questions:

How do you sell to your end-users?

Do you use a direct sales team, resellers, a website, or a combination thereof?

A sales force organization consists of a sales force that is structured in a way which will benefit the company, and ultimately the end-user. Some sales forces are highly structured while others are not. The best path depends on the organization, the context of your market — whether products or services — and how you see your organization meeting its objectives.

Product or service distribution constitutes one of the 4 P's in the marketing mix. In this case, it's the "place" or "placement" (aka distribution). It's a crucial factor in your entire marketing strategy as it helps you expand your reach and grow revenue in the most efficient manner. Deciding upon and plotting such a structure can be a daunting task in a company's strategic plan as there are several factors to consider — amongst them the geographical territory and type of customer.

STRUCTURING YOUR SALES ORGANIZATION

The sales structure should reflect strategy. A company's initial decision has to be about what channels are most efficient for reaching and serving the target customers and either:

- Your own direct salespeople; or

- Some combination of indirect sales organizations/ channel partners.

Will you use a combination of distributors, brokers, sales representative organizations, telemarketing, e-commerce/Internet, home-shopping TV channel(s) and distributors — retailers — or resellers?

Once you have chosen the appropriate combination of sales channels, the second decision is how to organize these channels by product line, major customer or market segment, function, geography, or no restrictions. This is referred to as sales force architecture.

Moving from the more general to the more specific, next decide how many salespeople you need and the boundaries of each person's territory. This is referred to as deployment and sizing.

Last and most tactical, a sales manager must assist salespeople in time and territory management. How can a salesperson best allocate his/her time in the territory between prospecting for new customers and further penetration of existing accounts? How frequently should top accounts be visited vs. less important customers?

What about product merchandising — should the salesperson also look after that task to assist the retailer with a higher sell-through? How can a salesperson most efficiently travel the territory?

CHANNEL CHOICE SUITABILITY

Choosing the proper distribution channels depends on several options.

Types of customers:

Certain customer characteristics lend themselves more to company direct salespeople, others to an independent sales organization. A large number of widely dispersed customers, frequently ordering small quantities, may be more efficiently reached by several outside indirect sales organizations than by your own company-employed direct sales force.

Based on certain metrics, present and potential accounts become designated A, B, or C. An A account requires more frequent calls than a C account and may require a different channel choice. You may use telesales people or e-commerce for C accounts and account representatives for B accounts.

Types of selling:

Certain types of selling should consider company direct salespeople, others, an indirect sales organization or a channel partner. Long sales cycles with a great deal of consultative selling to first-time or one-time systems buyers afford themselves to a direct sales organization. A channel partner may not have the patience for a long complex sale.

The more influence a salesperson has on the sale, the more important is the company direct sales force.

Team selling and partnership selling lend themselves to the company direct model. In contrast, relationship selling to repeat customers modified repeat buyers, display, commodity and order taking should consider using channel partners.

Types of products or services:
Certain types of products or services lend themselves to company direct salespeople, while others to indirect channel partners.

Heterogeneous products that can be more easily differentiated, such as bio-tech or consulting services or semiconductor fabricating equipment can utilize a direct company sales force. Homogeneous products or services that are more difficult to differentiate, such as injection molding, can utilize channel partners.

In reaching customers, higher gross margin products or services generally use a direct company sales force, while lower gross margin products or services generally use channel partners since their costs are lower and less fixed.

New products or services, where the salesperson has a strong influence on the sale, do best with a company direct sales force, while products or services toward the end of their life cycle are more efficiently handled by channel partners, telemarketing, e-commerce or consumer service people.

EFFICIENCY AND INCENTIVES DRIVE PRODUCTIVITY

No matter how well you hire, train and compensate salespeople, inefficient distribution channels, architecture, deployment and territory management will prevent a sales force from reaching full productivity. Salespeople represent an expensive and important human resource, just as plant and equipment represent expensive and important capital expenditures. Both require full productivity to be competitive.

With the sales force and distributors alike, keeping them stimulated is important. Positive motivators such as with sales contests are favored over low performance penalties such as reduced discounts and the threat of terminating the relationship.

Moreover, proper communication, mutually agreed sales goals, scheduled performance review meetings, reporting procedures (utilizing the CRM system), as well as collaborative marketing strategy, ongoing training, market intelligence information and being receptive to suggestions from the field for improvements all help.

There are also non-financial incentives which provide a form of intuitive type of income as opposed to financial income. Competitions, dinners, thank you letters and congratulatory awards all facilitate to keep everyone motivated and working closely together.

SALES OUTSOURCING: THE FLEXIBLE ALTERNATIVE

Given the competitive environment and emphasis on cost cutting at many firms, some organizations prefer to utilize sales outsourcing as a flexible and cost effective alternative.

A recent study has highlighted flexibility as an important driver for outsourcing sales (Rogers, B., 2009 – "*Contract sales organizations: making the transition from tactical resource to strategic partnering*").

Outsourcing the sales task does away with sales processes, targeting clients, hiring, as well as deploying a sales team, which is quite demanding and time consuming. This can help the company focus on their core products or services. Another attractive use of outsourcing is to test new markets, or to expand into distant markets without having to undergo an expensive geographic expansion.

This can lead to substantially increased sales through a multiple market presence. Companies may also choose sales outsourcing as a way to access the best sales skills.

In essence, the outsourcing firm known professionally as CSO (Contract Sales Organization) is an extension of their client but is responsible for all activities connected with direct sales activities, often receiving product/service knowledge training support from the client.

A prominent American outfit which offers such services boasts that by bringing together people, process and technology, it can help sales organizations:

- Design and deploy fully managed, highly skilled sales teams in weeks;

- Stimulate revenue streams, channel performance and business growth;

- Improve sales insight and reporting;

- Refine sales planning and strategies;

- Boost ROI and performance-to-budget.

Outsourcing isn't a good fit for every business. However, if you have more opportunities to sell your product than you can take advantage of, outsourcing can offer impressive growth. But its drawbacks can include the lack of control over execution, and the commission structure might be problematic. In addition, while sales outsourcing firms are hired by your company, they also represent numerous other companies, and as such may not be fully committed to you.

CHANNEL CONFLICTS

Be prepared for channel conflicts and have a plan for dealing with them. Today, e-commerce has become a more important distribution channel creating a new set of channel conflicts. Use e-commerce/Internet to enable your sales force and channel partners to embrace and benefit from it rather than compete with it.

When it comes to product/service pricing, by using multiple channels, make certain that a fair profit for each type of partner is included in the pricing. Compare the price that the end-user will pay. If a customer can buy from one channel at a lower price than another, your partners will have legitimate concerns. Pricing conflict is common, and it can jeopardize an entire strategy.

IN THE FINALE

Whether you create an in-house sales force, go with independent reps, or utilize a sales brokerage, each method has its key factors to consider.

As with in-house sales reps, channel partners require performance pay that rewards positive action and superior results are important for the success of your firm. Use proper training and compensation to prevent your channel partners from becoming adversaries.

Channel choices should be reviewed annually to see what has changed and if these changes require an adjustment in your choice of distribution. To make the proper channel choice, you must prioritize or rank the important issues relating to your organization.

Based on each issue's importance does this suggest a direct or indirect sales force — your own salespeople or a channel partner?

Essentially, to create an efficient distribution program, focus on the needs of your end-users while doing so in concert with your cost of sales, margin, and cash flow calculations. After all, you're in a for-profit business. Once you've chosen and created an "ideal" sales channel for your organization, you will need a sales process and a pricing strategy. Subsequently, you can begin launching marketing campaigns to channel partners and end-users.

"If you pick the right people and give them the opportunity to spread their wings and put compensation as a carrier behind it you almost don't have to manage them."

— Jack Welch

Sales Force Dynamics: Instituting an Ideal Compensation Plan

Sales compensation is a crucial factor in motivation. It is the sales executive's best strategic tool to drive sales performance and motivate specific selling behaviors. When designing sales compensation plans, one of the most important steps is to identify the appropriate measures on which your sales representatives will be paid. A combination of salary, commission and bonus is usually most effective. The question then becomes how to successfully blend all three that will entice achievers, as well as reward them according to performance. Nevertheless, the plan needs to be kept as simple as possible.

THE TOTAL COMPENSATION MIX: WHAT DOES IT ENTAIL?

Total compensation depends on the complexity of the salesperson's selling tasks. The mix between performance and fixed pay depends on:

1. Balancing salesperson and company needs;
2. The type of salesperson you want to attract;
3. The salesperson's influence on the sale;
4. The type of product or service sold; and
5. Rewarding the salesperson's specific actions or results most important to the company's success.

Sales force compensation involves not merely salary, commission and bonus but also fringe benefits and reimbursed expenses — though these last two are considered non-compensatory since they are not influenced by sales results.

An ideal compensation plan should:

- reward positive action and superior results important to the success of your company;
- the mix between fixed and performance pay should reflect the type salesperson you wish to attract and the salesperson's influence on the sales;
- the total level of compensation ought to reflect the complexity of the sale.

TYPES OF SALES FORCE COMPENSATION

DIRECT COMPENSATION consists of:

- Fixed pay (salary)
- Performance pay (commission)
- Deferred performance pay (bonus)
- Fringe benefits (Social security/insurance, group insurance, optional profit sharing etc.)
- Reimbursed expenses

CONSTRUCTING A TOTAL COMPENSATION PLAN

In constructing a compensation program, you first decide on the total dollars of compensation for a top salesperson in your industry — the "target" compensation. Your next decision is dividing those dollars between fixed and performance pay. The total compensation appropriate for a successful salesperson is determined by the complexity of the sale and type of selling. You define a "successful salesperson" as someone who ranks in the top 25 percent of your sales force in terms of results (based on annual dollars of sales or margin and growth). The following are simply a guideline.

- A successful/top salesperson involved in a long, complex, multi-step, consultative, partnership sales process should receive over US$100,000 (or your currency equivalent) annually in compensation regardless of the mix between fixed and performance pay.

- A salesperson involved in multi-level relationship sales, which includes the re-purchase of existing systems, which may require some post-sale service, generally receives US$60,000 to US$100,000 (or your currency equivalent) annually in total direct compensation regardless of the mix between fixed and performance pay. These people use more transactional sales to hunt or harvest and have titles such as "Territory Representative" or "Account Manager".

- A successful salesperson involved in route sales of homogeneous products or services, requiring a multitude of daily customer visits and feature selling and order taking from a person delegated by the buyer's decision maker generally receives under US$60,000 in total direct compensation, regardless of the mix between fixed and performance pay.

- Salespeople selling and servicing grocery stores with food products, drugstores and giftware, midsized businesses with temporary help services and manufacturers with die casting or injecting molding products generally receive annual direct compensation of under US$60,000 (or your currency equivalent).

Experience shows that more fixed dollars of compensation paid allows the management to more easily direct/control a salesperson.

SURVEYS EXPOSED

According to *Equation research*, their 3,000 respondent, 2005 sales compensation survey results indicated the following:

- Top sales people averaged with a total compensation of $157,234, midlevel performers with an average of $94,872 and low performers with $64,844.

- 50% to 60% of the total compensation was fixed pay for all three of the above groups.

In a 2009 *Watson Wyatt survey on sales force compensation and management* reveals that sales and HR executives (129 respondents), at a large cross-section of North American industries, are confident in the current alignment between sales performance and sales compensation. Seventy-nine percent report that their top performers earn the highest levels of sales compensation, indicating a strong link between pay and performance.

CORRECT MIX OF PERFORMANCE AND FIXED PAY

The mix between performance and fixed pay depends on:

1. **Balancing the company's and salespeople's needs** — *The company needs to attract, retain and motivate salespeople who produce a desired level of sales at a cost that generates profits and allows necessary percentage returns on sales and invested capital. It must reflect the company's culture, strategy and position on the growth curve.*

2. **The type of salesperson you want to attract** — *Fixed pay oriented compensation plans generally attract salespeople who are team players, ambitious to climb the executive ladder, steady rather than top performers, farmers rather than hunters and more comfortable selling presold products. On the other hand, Performance pay type compensation plans generally attract aggressive career sales-*

people, hunters rather than farmers and those with little ambition for promotion into management.

3. **The salesperson's influence on the sale** — *Ex: A company with all performance pay means the salesperson has a great deal or total influence on the sale.*

4. **The type of product or service sold** — *An order taker type of salesperson rather than an active seller, whereby he/she has less influence on the sale.*

5. **Rewarding the salesperson's specific actions or results most important to the company's success** — *The sales force compensation plan must reward actions and results on the part of salespeople that are most important to the company's success. Generally, a commission is used to reward results and a bonus is used to reward activities or exceeding goals. A group bonus might also be considered to reward teamwork.*

If salespeople have a pricing window and/or discretion to give discounts, allowances and promotions, a portion of their compensation should be based on dollars of gross margin rather than revenue for their territory. For example, a women's apparel manufacturer pays a commission rate on gross margin dollars because salespeople have some discretion to negotiate price.

To prevent making your compensation plan too complicated, limit the performance pay metrics to three actions or results — all of which are controllable by the individual.

It is suggested that each year, the company's sales leadership should re-evaluate the sales force compensation program as business constantly evolves.

NEW PRODUCT PLACEMENT

Many firms reward new product placement through their compensation plans. A salesperson exerts the most influence on a customer's decision during a product or service's introduction and the least during a product or service's decline. As such, some firms pay a higher level and rate of performance pay on new products and a lesser level and rate of performance pay on mature or declining products or markets.

TRANSACTIONAL VS. CONSULTATIVE SELLING

Salespeople involved in transactional sales will receive rewards in fewer performance areas than those involved in the more complex consultative sales. Salespeople involved in *farming* or maintenance will receive less variable pay than those involved in *hunting* or new account acquisition.

SUPPORT PERSONNEL

If your firm supports direct salespeople with product specialists, sales engineers or customer service representatives, consider performance pay for these people as it will encourage them to be team players for the good of the organization.

CHANNEL PARTNERS (OUTSIDE/INDEPENDENT REPRESENTATIVE ORGANIZATIONS)

Brokers, distributors and outside sales representative organizations generally receive 100 percent performance pay from the firms whose products they sell. However, channel partners need specific rewards for positive action and results important to the success of your company. For your indirect sales force to become partners rather than adversaries, they require training and correct monetary incentives. Apply the same criteria for your indirect sales force that you did for your direct people. Generally, your channel partners compensate their salespeople with a plan similar to the one you use to compensate the channel partners.

CHANGE MANAGEMENT AND IMPLEMENTATION

One way to sell compensation changes to the sales force involves including them in the decision-making process. Select a representative group to participate in the analysis, suggest changes and anticipate problems. Address concerns by showing how the new compensation plan can increase annual pay. Annual performance changes must be announced before the year begins so that salespeople have time to adjust their thinking activities.

WHEN IT'S ALL SAID AND DONE

Sales compensation is a tricky business as there are a number of payment models to choose from and each method has its pros and cons. Commissions motivate employees to sell harder, while salaries create loyal employees. To attract, motivate and retain the best salespeople, you pay them what they are worth. Performance pay that rewards positive action along with results can create windfall earnings for salespeople and increased revenues for the company. However, in the end, it is the sales manager's job to make the salespeople successful so that they can fully monetize on the reward plan.

"If you don't know where you are going, you will probably end up somewhere else."

— Laurence J Peter

Management by Tactics : A Sales Management Supervisory Technique and its Effects on Sales Performance

Ask any person involved in a sales supervisory position what they consider a salesperson's most important daily task and you will most likely receive the same response: "Sales/Prospecting Activities".

Although most companies monitor and make efforts to control sales activities, few companies have a formal means of optimizing tactics. Leaders should take the time and effort to design performance measurement systems that are based on a balanced set of metrics and then reward their sales reps based on the desirable behaviors and the positive outcomes that result.

MANAGEMENT BY TACTICS: THE INPUT FOCUSED PROTOCOL

Management by Tactics or MBT is a term, that describes a supervisory technique applied by progressive sales management. A Canadian sales strategist, Dr. Giovanni Di Girolamo, along with his associate consultants, conceived it in 2005. Through their research and personal experiences, they discovered a process, that consistently yielded unsurpassed results from sales representatives — regardless of industry, sales experience or type of client (new or existing).

The principle behind this is a process where sales managers/directors, along with their sales force, identify the day-to-day activities required to achieve sales objectives and focus their energies in controlling such activities (known as "input") – rather than simply focusing on results (a.k.a. "output").

The latter applies to Management by Objectives or MBO, a technique first popularized by the late management guru, Peter Drucker, which places a great deal of emphasis on the outputs — in our case, the sales results.

TACTICS VS. STRATEGY

A tactic equates to an action plan for attaining a particular goal. The terms "tactic" and "strategy" are often confused: tactics are the actual means used to gain an objective, while strategy is the overall campaign plan, which may involve complex operational patterns, activity, and decision-making that lead to tactical execution.

RESEARCH AND CONSEQUENCES

The research that was conducted in a 12-month period, by the Canadian sales strategist and his team, consisted of twenty-nine subjects from a sample of four companies representing different types of industries. During this study, sales representatives from the four companies worked exclusively with output goals — namely sales objectives. Data were collected. This stage of the research was referred to as the "Pre-Test".

The researcher then proceeded to implement the Management by Tactics method. In this phase of the research, the salespeople were given input goals, such as the number of telephone calls to be made, number of prospects to visit along with various sales presentations to be performed. This stage of the research was referred to as the "Post-Test".

Results from all four companies indicated that MBT had a positive impact on sales performance. The outcome was as follows:

- In the absence of applying MBT, all representatives in the study under achieved sales objectives by between 21% to 75% of their target.

- On the other hand, when all sales reps were given input goals under the MBT system, the weakest sales rep attained 100% of target — while the other two reached 117% and 118% respectively for a combined average of 112% of sales targets.

OBSERVATIONS AND EFFECT

Management by Objectives (MBO) is a results-oriented management system, whereby; top management involvement in the process is crucial along with employee agreement to the same organizational objectives. In sales, the manager and salesperson identify and negotiate specific goals for the upcoming period. Subsequently, the sale rep and manager sign a performance agreement that specifies these goals as performance standards. In contrast, Management by Tactics (MBT) focuses on the effort and activities by adopting the following philosophy:

- Activity information and feedback encourages greater incentive and effort.

- Micro-management equals detail oriented, whereas, macro-management

- equals the big picture.

- Behavior oriented salespeople outperform the results oriented type.

- Clarity of tasks to be accomplished and feedback are two key factors at motivating salespeople. Link rewards to performance.

- Activity reports should be submitted by the salespeople and reviewed by sales management during scheduled coaching sessions. These include:
    1. Weekly activity report;
    2. Observation report (is used to evaluate the salesperson's overall ability to perform the job and includes various factors crucial in obtaining results);
    3. Annual evaluation form.

No doubt, we have all heard the expression from various management authorities, "What gets measured, gets done." Sales leaders and their sales force should focus on the process/activities rather than the end result, as output control has no direct effect on end performance. By working backwards, namely, taking the desired output and breaking it into activities required to achieve the output or end result, has been proven to be the most practical approach.

"The majority of men meet with failure because of their lack of persistence in creating new [sale management] plans to take the place of those which fail."

— Napoleon Hill

Sales Management: Focusing On Core Competencies for Extraordinary Results

When Faddy Sidaros, a Regional Sales Director for Pitney Bowes Canada, was asked what he considers to be his biggest challenges, his emphatic response was: "Coaching the coach to be on the same wavelength and linking the sales representatives' personal goals to those of the company."

There is no doubt that sales are the heart and soul of any public or private enterprise. It's about the need for a constant stream of new business, which brings in the necessary cash flow. This should explain why nothing happens until a sale is made. That simple point underscores the critical importance of sales to the business — regardless of its size. However, in today's global marketplace, owners and managers face many challenges related to fulfilling the customer's ever-changing needs and expectations. With that come refined methods of selling a product or service to a well-informed and discerning customer — especially with the advent of the information age and plethora of choices.

Sales management can be most easily defined as planning, implementing, and controlling personal contact programs designed to achieve the sales and profit objectives of the firm. Overall, sales managers and sales directors are responsible for leading the firm's sales program. More specifically, they are accountable to reviewing and analyzing sales performance against programs, quotas and plans to determine effectiveness. To excel in those areas requires discipline, planning, executing, as well as frequent checks and balances.

BUSINESS DEVELOPMENT AND ACCOUNT MANAGEMENT: WHAT DO THEY REALLY SIGNIFY?

Business development is about techniques and responsibilities which aim at gaining new customers and at penetrating existing markets. Given that the title "Sales Representative" on business cards and in casual conversations may be perceived negatively, there are businesses that have replaced the traditional title for their representatives with "Business Development". This is merely image sprucing for the salesperson. In spite of this, the end result is to make sales rather than merely develop business.

Account Management, according to businessdictionary.com, is defined as, "An employee who is tasked with day-to-day support of a particular customer's account with a business, and who serves as the primary point of contact between the customer and the company. The account manager position can provide customer support, technical support, planning and optimization for the account, as well as developing a relationship with the customer."

"Consultative Sales", on the other hand is what all salespeople should be striving for. The days of pushing for the close through high pressure techniques has been replaced with a method, which educates and guides a client who will be making a sound purchase because it will fulfill a practical need. It's now the logical purchase decision vs. strictly the emotional.

B2B VS. B2C — THE DIFFERENCE IS IN THE SALES PROCESS

Selling to B2B customers can be accomplished through a direct sales force or a channel sales force. The biggest difference in the two is the time frame from start of a sale to the close of a sale. Typically B2B requires more time than B2C, though there are exceptions to every rule. For this reason, the methods and approaches used by the salespeople are different.

SALES VS. MARKETING — THE LATTER COMPLEMENTS THE FORMER

Marketing and selling are two different things. Selling focuses on closing the deal, often as quickly as possible. Marketing is about developing an image and a presence in the market place and ensuring that people know about your company/organization. Marketing is a longer-term activity and requires an investment of both time and energy. Both of these should work in harmony and by strategically combining both efforts, a business will experience a successful amount of growth. A salesperson can be provided with real-time insights and marketing support that can be beneficial to, the company's reputation in retaining, cross selling and up-selling the customer profitably.

RECRUITING HIGH CALIBER SALESPEOPLE FOR A QUICK START AND SUSTAINED GROWTH

There are few challenges in trying to recruit an effective sales force. Because of its impact on the company's bottom line, selecting the right salespeople is a critical area that requires a lot of attention. Kelly Parker Hanna, a marketing and business development strategist with Key Group management consulting, summarizes the hiring dilemma this way:

"I think that managers have a tough time identifying if they are hiring a star to begin with. If the sales manager would have potential hires take a sales assessment, they could weed out the people who may not do well in the job."

Seeking potential sales-oriented candidates begins with a qualifications criterion, which can be translated into a final job description, along with where to actually look for them. Always start by working with referrals and your networking group rather than delve right into ad/job boards. Interviewing should be conducted by the sales manager and avoided by anyone else unfamiliar with the sales task such as a human resources staffer — as is usually the case.

A potential new salesperson's most telling first test is selling himself/herself to you. Interviewers should look for three characteristics that will tip them off to a promising new representative including presentation, personality, and a track record of sales success. If one wants to take it one step further, the candidate can be asked to complete a profile assessment/questionnaire. Recent validation studies and thousands of observed experiences prove that personality traits give managers an advantage in hiring salespeople who can meet and exceed expectations. Last but not least, the prospective salesperson should believe in the product or service he/she will be selling, as well as fit within the organization's culture.

TRAINING, DEVELOPMENT & COACHING: MANAGING SALESPEOPLE BY MANAGING THEIR ACTIVITIES

Nowadays, customers expect salespeople to be more knowledgeable, respond faster and provide value-added, customized solutions to their problems. To accomplish this, salespeople must develop closer, longer-term relationships with their customers than in the past. Given that the demands of the job have changed, it follows that the type of person the organization selects for this job and the training he or she receives must also adapt with the times.

Companies should not hesitate to invest resources with structured and ongoing training/development programs for their sales staff. These include a new sales recruit orientation curriculum, a comprehensive sales assessment, targeted training activities, real-world applications and one-on-one coaching. The sales manager can be given the task of training or if the organization is large enough, a dedicated trainer will be undertaking such a task. However, the sales manager is the person who is solely responsible for one-on-one coaching of his/her respective salespeople, which should be performed at least once per week.

Training subjects should place emphasis on:

1. Ways to increase client numbers and revenue

2. Understanding the marketing processes better by including a SWOT Analysis;

3. Systematizing the sales (and marketing process) to reliably generate additional new inquiries;

The salesperson would be at an advantage concentrating on activities, such as making calls, rather than on sales objectives. As a result, the salesperson's motivation will be higher, hence, better results. Managing salespeople by managing their activities (a.k.a. Management by Tactics or "MBT") is a process, which has been proven to create a positive effect on sales performance.

COLD CALLING: PROSPECTING HARD VS. PROSPECTING SMART

The old school of thought on the subject of prospecting continues to exist today. There are still too many Sales VPs, Directors, C-level execs, and peddlers of out-dated sales books, who insist upon more cold calls. In this day-and-age, cold-calling does not make sense especially when we consider that technology and consumers themselves have evolved. Likewise, there are far better ways for you to communicate with prospects in a less frustrating and obnoxious way.

It is no longer acceptable or wise to randomly call a business professional. They are far too busy to waste time dealing with interruptions. This strengthens the reason for Sales to work intimately with Marketing to create lead-generating sources.

The following modern day effective prospecting techniques can be applied in lieu of cold calling:

1. **Referrals** from existing clients or spheres of influence. A referral gift program can be created and promoted to existing clientele and perhaps others.

2. **Pre-approach/warm-up letters** to specific/named decision makers with a promise to do a follow-up call days later.

3. **The Internet** — Exposure and lead generation from the company's Website and third party sites. Google Ad-words, Search Engine Optimization (SEO), affiliate marketing, and banner ads.

4. **Trade-Show Presence/Participation** with leads to be processed and followed-up.

5. **Direct Mail & Special Offer Campaigns** created by the marketing staff. The campaigns should involve multiple touches over a specific period with strong calls-to-action.

6. **Attend Networking Events** locally and beyond (depending on sales territory).

7. **Social Media:** Uncover and engage with prospects. It's surprising how many people are on Twitter and LinkedIn discussing problems a salesperson can solve and inquiring about what is sold. Reaching-out to them and finding ways to help works, although with time-consuming results.

SALES STRUCTURE = POLICIES, GUIDELINES, PROCEDURES & TOOLS

In any organization, let alone in the sales division, without any sort of structure the chances of failure increases. By clearly defining the structure of a sales team, a business ensures that each and every member of the sales force knows his/her boundaries, responsibilities and duties. The structure of the sales team to a great extent depends on the number of people in the sales force.

In a small organization with just a few sales employees, it is essential not to draw too many boundaries because then you will need to hire additional staff to do the work that is left over. However in a larger organization it is important that structural lines are clearly drawn so that no one steps on another's toes.

SALES COMPENSATION: CREATING A WIN-WIN FORMULA

Since no two companies are alike, a sales-driven compensation plan can vary from one organization to the next. However, the following factors should be taken into account when devising a win-win payment reward plan:

- Industry (B2B or B2C);
- Sales cycle;
- Deal sizes;
- Sales type (group sale, consultative, one-on-one);
- Industry knowledge;
- Inbound lead quality.

The two emotions that drive most sales representatives are fear and greed. For this reason, the easiest way to motivate them is to structure their compensation plan accordingly. For the most part, this will include a reasonable basic salary along with a sliding commission scale, based on volume and/or size of a deal, including a quarterly, semi-annual or annual bonus depending upon a set quota.

EXPLOITING TECHNOLOGY AND CRM: VITAL ASSETS FOR SALES EFFICIENCY

When it comes to Customer Relationship Management, (CRM) software/tools, the data, analytics and technology are merely tools that should be used only after the customer-centric culture is embedded within the sales force and the organization itself. A properly implemented CRM system such as *Sales Force* can bring significant benefits to organizations. The system/application covers the so-called 3 "P"'s as in People (employees and culture), Procedures (way of doing business) and Programs (supporting applications) – not just an application running on a computer.

The practicalities of the technology used are many and varied. Tools such as wireless computing, mobile telephony and "cloud computing" can increase efficiency. As well as providing access to the information, they need to accelerate the sales process. In addition, the sales force can be kept connected to the office, update information automatically, deliver required information promptly and enable mobile order placement and signature capture. This undoubtedly makes the sales job easier, so representatives/account managers can focus on what they do best, and in the process, enhance customer service.

OUTSOURCING SALES MANAGEMENT: A SOLUTION FOR SMALL AND MEDIUM SIZE COMPANIES

If sales are not an enterprise's core competency, particularly in the start-up phase, or if it's ready to expand to the next level of corporate growth, then outsourcing the sales management function should be considered. Like so, owners can focus their time and resources on their main capabilities — most notably their products/services and operating issues.

This solution would alleviate the pressure to deal with developing sales processes and hiring a sales team. By outsourcing this, a company will be able to progress more rapidly by getting the sales execution focus from an outside experienced sales director. Furthermore, this can be accomplished for a fraction of the monthly cost of full time hire and without a permanent obligation.

PUTTING IT ALL TOGETHER

Consider a sales force that behaves more like "consultative agents" instead of aggressive peddlers. Along with the thorough knowledge of the company's products/services, the charismatic, enthusiastic, motivated and competent sales force should be constantly trained, developed and coached — along with all the necessary tools at their possession for added competitiveness. Salespeople should be client centered. That is, focus on needs/wants and fulfill them with specific products/services — solutions.

This is how trust will be earned. Clients don't like being sold to — they prefer to buy (push vs. pull). Businesses ought to know their ideal customer/target market, the competition and how they can be approached most effectively. The sales force should not have to resort to the daily grind of making cold calls. Instead, they can be provided with techniques and tools to make better use of their prospecting time. In the end, more of their valuable time can be spent in the field in front of prospective clients rather than working on the law of averages in search of appointments.

Better still; the lead-generation activity can be outsourced to a company specializing in those services. Marketing should collaborate closely with Sales on a mutual goal. Management focusing on activities and results can through its place and its data constantly monitor a simple to use yet comprehensive CRM system.

"Any damn fool can put on a deal, but it takes genius, faith and perseverance to create a brand."

— David Ogilvy

"If, in the business of communication, image is king, the essence of this image, the logo, is the jewel in its crown".

— Paul Rand

Chapter IV: Marketing and Branding Tactics

Branding Strategies for a Fundamental Differentiation

Most businesses have an opinion on what branding constitutes, though how do you go about standing out from similar product or service categories? Let us first look at the Cambridge English Dictionary definition of "Branding". It is "the act of giving a company a particular design or symbol in order to advertise its products and services." Sounds very simplistic. However, we know that it takes plenty of thought, creativity and flawless execution to truly define a brand which radiates externally to produce notable customer experiences. A brand is essentially an intangible asset which is injected with personality — values that consumers like and can relate to. Moreover, a cleverly created and executed branding strategy develops an intangible association with consumers.

DEFINING THE BRAND

We start with the idea of what we want the product, service and its respective company to be perceived as. What do you want it to represent? Specifically what category does it belong to that will be in the consumers' minds? Defining your target market too will help to strengthen the brand's effectiveness. Explain what your brand stands for and why it is better than the competition. This is where you execute your brand communications. Commonly used methods of brand communications include advertising, events, sponsorships, promotions, direct marketing, customer relationship management programs and public relations. In defining who your brand and your audience are, you create the foundation for all other components to build on. This requires a distinctive brand vision, positioning, personality and affiliation for the product/service. Those are crucial factors that will make it truly unique. Proper branding can also get you out of the commodity trap and attract value in terms of higher pricing.

CUSTOMER EXPERIENCES

This is what truly creates differentiation from mass and from competing brands. The key objective is to create a relationship of trust. The world's powerful brands establish trust and friendship with their customers. They develop emotional capital, and gain passion. This is what makes them great. A brand's image is how consumers perceive it and this may not be the same as how the owner wants it to be seen. It is important to note that without a premium product or service quality, a strong brand image is difficult to create.

Every customer contact ("touch points") should be handled with the utmost care to ensure that the total brand experience a person has is consistent. This involves properly training and occasionally evaluating employee performance and when necessary, changing strategy, systems, technology, methods, services, products and even physical premises to produce a positive customer experience. Complacency should be replaced with continuous improvement.

STANDING-OUT FROM THE CROWD

Brands can't stand out by blending in. They need to be distinctive, compelling, create buzz and call for action. Advertising in almost every industry appears to look the same. Visually distinctive brand features enhance customer recall and positively influence intent to purchase. "Advertising" creates attention and promotes an image and the brand. On the other hand, "Marketing" compels someone to buy. Since we're constantly bombarded with advertising, it's important to cut through the clutter. You only have one or two seconds to grab the attention of your intended audience. Compared to your competition, take an unusual approach by being first, different and bold in the way you create and deliver your message.

Marketing campaigns should have elements of:

- Imagination;
- Mystery;
- Memory.

Whether a product or service is a luxury brand or falls into another category, it is how you stand out from the crowd that distinguishes you.

Know your target audience, get inside their heads and understand how they think and feel. What are their fears, emotions and anxieties? It's not just about demographics; it's about neuro-psychology. Once you have this done pat, you then manage the brand consistently.

"What's a brand? A singular idea or concept that you own inside the mind of the prospect."

— Al Ries

Professional Branding Up Close and Personal: Advice for the Private Practice

For a professional in private practice, the notion of marketing and branding is unfamiliar territory. This is in a similar situation as within any small entrepreneurial company. Yet, this is truly a fundamental aspect of any business. To develop a following requires a brand, and it doesn't matter if you are a doctor, dentist, an accountant, or an attorney. Your personal "brand" is what comes to mind when your "clients" are deciding whether to see you for the first or not.

Now is the time to get real. Branding is about image and perception. Do not claim not to understand the social networks. Muck right in, but with a special eye to product awareness. Hear yourself scream out, Facebook, LinkedIn, Twitter and Google Trends, here I come!

In principle, a brand is a promise of something that will be delivered by you and your practice. This promise comes in a form of quality, an experience, as well as with a certain expectation in mind. Brands that stand for something connect with customers.

Just as you use brands to personify your position, status, and identity when you make decisions about which detergent or automobile to buy so do your clients. Give them something to rely on, something they can sink their teeth into, something which enhances their identity with a positive vibe.

Your credentials have much to do with your image in the consumer's mind, so does your office ambiance and the courtesy (or lack of) offered the minute your staff greet the patient/client at the front desk. You may also be the doctor with bad breath or architect who is frequently late for appointments.

CONCEPTUAL PERSONAL BRANDING

Branding is similar to the development of our own personal traits. Our looks, the clothes we wear, our personality, achievements, contacts, experiences and anything else that adds to, or even detracts from, our appeal to others encompasses our own "personal brand."

When branding your own private practice, you have the ability to carefully create a brand position that will appeal to your market and make your profession more successful through broader, or in some cases, very specific appeal. However, brand development requires time, energy, as well as a reasonable budget.

Personal brand positioning is the activity of creating an identity with a distinctive value in the target customer's mind. For instance, when we think of an accomplished defense attorney, the first ones that spring to mind are those who have a reputation for having a high rate of litigation success — or cardiologists who are identified as utterly competent in curing most heart diseases and extending their patients' life span. Essentially that is the position they occupy in your mind whenever you think of them.

PACKAGE YOURSELF AS "THE" ENTITY

A sound marketing and branding plan can help make your clients/patients feel confident about your practice. In addition, a sound sustained campaign will help get new ones to grow your practice. Doing so requires the following action plan which will help build your name in a professional and unique way that enhances your recognition, and trust and confidence in you as a physician, attorney, architect or other licensed professional.

There are several tactics in creating an effective personal brand. These include:

- **Enhance your Competitive Edge**

  By building a strong personal brand you are creating a sense of individuality and "distinctiveness" in the marketplace so that your clients are able to easily differentiate your practice from your competitors.

- **Make the Big Leap**

  Your professional brand becomes your authentic personal identity. The goal of personal branding is to create and portray a consistent image of what you are as a person and what you stand for. It's a reflection of you which includes your values, opinions, and beliefs that are determined by what you say do, and how you do it.

- **Create Awareness**

  Due to the plethora of similar products and services offered in the marketplace, consumers are now placing more emphasis on brand differentiation when it comes to distinguishing comparable products and services. As a services professional, you have the ability to take control of your identity and influence the perception others will have about you and the services you offer.

- **Create the Buzz**

  Effortless business growth can be achieved by exploiting word-of-mouth advertising through clients/patients, as well as various networks that the buzz spreads through. The latter will be produced when your personal brand will connect you with your spheres of influence who will send you referrals and give you testimonials.

The idea is to give people a reason to talk about you in a flattering way which is considered customer-to-customer selling. Your personal brand should be communicated consistently through many channels which will begin to generate the hype and create excitement for your practice.

A case in point: A dentist in an affluent suburb of Montreal has distinguished himself and his practice from other dental offices in the area by having instilled a mission statement that he and his staff abide by vigorously. This includes guests welcomed in a friendly and state-of-the-art facility with a Zen ambiance to guarantee that each patient visit to the office is both relaxing and enjoyable with the most extraordinary care in the dental field.

The attractive website even includes a 360 degree tour of the premises which is quite impressive. The dentist is renowned for perpetually honing his skills through continuing education and latest techniques, as well as for his high level of patient satisfaction. As a result, it is believed that the majority of new patients come through word-of-mouth.

- **Generate Profitability in Less Time**

    A highly regarded personal brand offers the advantage of attracting clients/patients in a timely and effortless manner. You will be able to position yourself in the mind of your typical client or patient as the expert of choice. In doing so, you begin to dominate your local market and command higher fees that, consequently translate into less work and more money — work smarter as opposed to harder.

- **Establish Celebrity Status**

    Gain name recognition in your area of expertise in your "customer's" mind. By making a lasting impression you will be well-rewarded for your distinctiveness. Trust, respect, and admiration will follow, and you will be perceived as an expert the more visible you are to your target audience. As a result, your brand will propel you to the top in your domain.

A specialist physician who has succeeded in becoming a celebrity in his own right is, undoubtedly, the well-publicized American Plastic Surgeon Dr. Robert M. Rey. His media appearances, starring role in the reality show Dr. 90210, his public relations savvy, VIP patient testimonials, as well as his exceptionally resourceful website all speak volumes of his strong personal brand — he is the ultimate self-promoter.

CREATE & SUSTAIN BRAND ONLINE

Begin by crafting a marketing, advertising and publicity campaign that focuses on helping you achieve your vision. Your consistent message should include your credentials, areas of specialization, as well as the ambiance and experience you desire to achieve for each and every client/patient. It is important to note that your local professional practice code of ethics in advertising may have some restrictions in place with regards to the content of your marketing and PR campaign.

The following greatly enhances your personal brand through the image you want to portray.

- **Marketing Collateral**

    Design an attractive yet professional looking logo and develop graphic standards for fonts and branding colors. Design consistent and matching corporate material which comprises your business card, letterhead, envelope, signage, brochures, note pads, newsletters, etc.

- **Waiting Room Ambiance**

    First impressions count, and so does comfort and the entire "customer" experience. Avoid being frugal with your image and invest in designing your office and in particular the waiting room to higher standards. This area speaks volumes about you, and this includes clean premises.

- **Website and Social Networking**

    Your website is essentially your online office and marketing presentation. It too conveys a strong message about your brand image. Make certain it is done professionally, free of any clutter, and includes the right amount of information — and make it effortless to navigate.

As for social networking profiles such as LinkedIn, ensure that you have a presence. Keep them current and don't mix any personal information or photos.

- **Trained and Courteous Staff**

    Branding goes beyond design, it also applies to your support staff. Since it's a given that your clients/patients are the lifeblood of your practice, it's not enough to simply take care of them with expert care and advice but also through excellent and courteous office and billing support. You and your staff are part of your brand, therefore choose them carefully, train them as often as possible and keep them motivated to excel.

BE MULTIDIMENSIONAL

You've spent years studying to earn your credentials whilst you learned about your specialization. Once you're ready to apply the knowledge as a self-employed professional, you discover that growing your practice requires you to compete with other offices to get new clients/patients and referrals.

Just as you are prepared to serve them you also have the extra burden of having to deal with self-branding and marketing issues — as any competent sole proprietorship should. A sound marketing and branding plan can help you grow your practice by attracting, as well as retaining clients/patients by making them feel confident about you.

Personal brand positioning should convey to your audience your unique/distinctive advantages over the competition, and while you are serving them, you are keeping your promise of delivering constantly across all points of contact. That's how trustworthy brands are built.

"Improving your brand is an investment in building your personal profile, reputation and the results you will achieve."

— Rachel Quilty

ME, Inc. : The Impact of Personal Branding in Strategic Marketing

I had a striking and might I say, haunting thought that continues to stick with me. Some time ago, I met a girlfriend through a dating site. Yes, I know this is not unusual. However, she once remarked that I marketed myself online like I was a "product". Through that pleasant conversation, I wasn't certain if this was to be construed as a compliment or a criticism. Although this hadn't been a calculated approach, I now understood the power of personal branding.

Today, personal branding is ubiquitous and an essential part of professional and non-professional activity. It isn't different from product branding and relies on the same critical and analytical eye and criteria to float the "product" in the market. The only difference is that the product in question is "you".

For example, if you are in the job market, the commodity you are selling is "you". This also applies if you are seeking a promotion within your organization or whether you're selling/categorizing yourself as the ideal independent consultant or political candidate respectively. The motives can be one or several.

THE BRAND CALLED "(PLACE YOUR FULL NAME HERE)"

No matter what your name is or who you are, you are engaged in selling an image you wish to portray to a targeted audience. Joe McGinnis in his cutting edge book "*The Selling of the President*" showed how this could be done effectively. The book focuses on how Richard Nixon was able to "sell" his profile to the American public in 1968.

As individuals, celebrities have pretty much mastered the art of turning themselves into powerful, eye-catching and memorable personal brands. Think Paris Hilton, Madonna, George Clooney, and Donald Trump. Even Barack Obama demonstrated how to take an unknown quantity and build a persuasive persona.

WHAT CAN WE LEARN FROM THEM?

To start with, it's not a one-off event but rather an on-going process. Companies constantly bombard us with messages and adverts for precisely this reason. To keep us reminded of their brand and thus reinforce their brand equity.

Keeping it genuine and delivering on promises is an equally important factor to consider. Your attitude and actions, from start to finish with any task you perform, sets the tone for the type of individual you are and what others can expect from you.

CREATE A BRAND STATEMENT AND A VALUE PROPOSITION

Marketers, most notably, product brand managers, create messages about their products or services that encourage us to buy. Those messages tell us attributes about the product and the benefits to us as consumers if we purchase their products/services. Likewise, as a personal brand, you need to develop at least one message about yourself that tells your target market what you bring to the table, the benefits they receive from doing business with you, as well as what attracts them to you.

Your value proposition is all about your competitiveness and should spell-out the strengths that surpass your competition.

To put your brand to work for you in your job search, you'll need to pull together all the pieces that make up your value proposition in the marketplace. A vibrant personal brand statement makes it that much easier for those assessing you to get an indication of what you bring to the organization.

EFFECTIVE COMMUNICATION ENHANCES YOUR BRAND

Whether you're a CEO, manager, consultant, entrepreneur, business owner, professional or even a job seeker, you should have the ability to persuade through your written and verbal messages. This includes giving effective interviews. Effective presentation skills will not only help you sell your ideas and products, but it will elevate your personal brand.

Management guru, Peter Drucker once stated, "As you move one step up from the bottom, your effectiveness depends on your ability to reach others through the spoken and written word."

This effective quotation not only tells it as it is, it also tells us a lot about Peter Drucker as an effective management expert and communicator.

CHARACTER VS. REPUTATION

Reputation is what people say or think about you. That's your personal brand and should be well-preserved. Character, on the other hand, is what you really are. It is crucial that you understand the distinction. It is said that character is like a tree and reputation like a shadow. The shadow is what we think of it; the tree is the real thing. Always deliver on what you promise and if you look after your character, your reputation will look after itself.

WHAT DOES PERSONAL BRANDING ENTAIL?

For personal branding to be effective, it requires managing perceptions effectively. This encompasses several characteristics including:

- **Be Unique and Remarkable** in what you do by differentiating yourself from the mainstream. In today's crowded and competitive world, we need that extra something that sets-us apart. Be distinctive, daring and acquire a competitive edge. After all, it's a "dog-eat-dog" environment and survival of the fittest. No matter what you do, you don't have to live your life the way other people expect you to.

- **Grooming and Clothes:** — They are the packaging of your total image. The way you dress and groom says a great deal about you — whether you're doing so out of necessity or doing it with flair, one can usually distinguish the difference. Watching your appearance also makes you feel good about yourself.

- **Etiquette:** — It forms a part of human interaction skills, is a strong indication of a refined person and proper upbringing. It should be applied in everyday life in a civilized society. In addition, Respect is esteem of a person, a personal quality and ability to demonstrate it to others through deeds.

SOCIAL NETWORKING: IS IT GOING TO BE FACEBOOK, LINKEDIN OR BOTH?

LinkedIn is the number one professional network, whereas, Facebook is presently the largest personal network with over 750 million active users worldwide. Each has its unique purpose. Whether you're a job seeker, consultant, and entrepreneur or happily employed, LinkedIn can be an incredible asset for your career or business. You can connect to over 100 million professionals in over 200 countries around the world. This is a cyber venue where a polished profile with a professional looking photo and error free text should be the only acceptable standard. It's a portrait of you and your brand. It's also where you will be importing your contacts and growing your network through new connections. In contrast to LinkedIn, Facebook is geared more toward socializing purposes with friends, relatives and acquaintances. Many companies are also taking serious notice whose idea is to engage with present and prospective clients.

It's equally important that you are prudent and selective with the type of content and photos you place on your page as anyone can come upon it through searches. The message your page conveys will either be positive or unfavorable to your image. Frequent verification and updates on both social networks is recommended. Otherwise, your profiles become stale and unattractive.

BLOGGING

Another powerful marketing tool to consider is a blog. Writing articles for your own blog and for others will earn you consideration as a respected expert in your industry and subject matter, which, taken together, will create more credibility for you and increase your presence on the Internet.

Regardless of the business you're in or message you're trying to depict to your audience, if you're going to successfully shape your brand, you need to start by knowing who you genuinely are, then form the image you want to present, and subsequently, behave the part consistently.

Everyone, it seems, has a personal brand, but most people are not aware of this and as a result do not manage it strategically, consistently, and effectively. As your own "brand," you are the head of "Me Inc."

How does it feel to be the CEO of your own brand and life?

"Business has only two functions - marketing and innovation."

— Milan Kundera

Exploiting the Benefits of Niche Marketing: Strategic Marketing

In strategic marketing "speak", who earns more money: a general practitioner or a specialist physician such as an ophthalmologist? The latter has spent additional years studying with emphasis in one particular area of practice which makes him/her both scarce and sought after in his/her profession. The same goes for an organization that has spent years studying the market with emphasis on doing one thing, but one thing extremely well. This automatically justifies higher fees translating to improved earnings. How does a saddle maker to the horse and carriage trade reposition itself to maximize its know-how in leather goods to now ask US$4,500 for a simple briefcase? Or even hawk silk scarves at US$400? Think of Hermes.

The answer lies in specialization, craftsmanship, and branding.

As with all other specialized professions, a business that, chooses to concentrate on a particular market segment should simply be generating higher revenues.

Alternatively, if you join the herd of the mainstream, there is always a vast consumer audience to tap. Profit is driven by volumes. It is harder to compete on price to the point of being perceived as offering a commodity with little or no differentiation — otherwise known as a "unique selling proposition" (USP). The only exception to that rule is when an enterprise keeps churning out innovative, "must have" items ahead of its competition. Yet that requires constant creativity, refinements, and a considerable amount of R&D. Apple is an example of a firm that has managed to hit both objectives. Not bad for an enterprise, that started life in a garage.

DEFINING THE "NICHE"

Strategically, niche marketing is the way to go forward. However, you must be on top of game. Recently, the firm *Kusmi Tea* has managed to put all the right elements together in an unbeatable combination. It personifies mass marketing and branding. If you have a specific group of people interested in "organic tea", you have your proverbial niche. Whether promoting niche products, in focused markets, such as those for vegans, cruises exclusively for "cougars and cubs" or geared for the ultra high net worth individuals, the activities applied to attract those refined target undoubtedly call for creative strategic thinking.

TARGETED AUDIENCES

The best way to start is to define your target audience. An 18-year-old girl who wants to lose weight to fit into her dress is interested in weight loss diets. Hit her at her waist line, and the target is captured with simplicity.

The family who just purchased a puppy wants it trained and therefore requires the appropriate service. Show you can make a dog shake, rattle, and roll and still act well-behaved in the company of others and you will no longer need to flog dog whistles.

Every notice how a 50-year-old lady wants to hide her wrinkles and is always searching for a miracle formula to make her wrinkles disappear in minutes? Open Vogue and see how this "class act" can be achieved. These cited groups above represent finely honed targeted audiences. Marketing to such audiences and building an emotional bridge from the intention to purchase decision always attracts higher conversions. You don't need to recreate the wheel. All you need to do is to find a suitable product that your target audience is looking for and present it on a silver platter. All target audiences liked to be addressed with intimacy and personal contact.

DRIVING THE NICHE

Common sense tells you that driving a selected audience is efficient and lucrative.

The following key index shows how niche marketing should be your chosen business strategy:

1. When entering new niche market, generally you will not have much competition to deal with. This is justification alone for choosing a specific market in the first place. It also makes your SEO (Search Engine Optimization) Internet marketing strategy focused and cost effective.

2. Niche markets appeal to target customers, and they are generally much more willing to spend money when their specific needs are met. This means that by catering to a specific target market, you can generally earn a better profit margin.

3. Some niche markets contain sub-groups of the main niche. For example, *acai* berry weight loss pills or natural weight loss diets are sub niches from the weight loss niche. Despite their relatively small size, they are actually quite sought after. Identifying this need spares you from having to compete for similar business. People who fit this profile will seriously consider your product — especially if it offers them a genuine solution.

4. Niche marketing makes it possible to focus on becoming a true expert within a particular realm while building a reputable brand name. Strategically, it is also more focused and easier to segment and attack.

CASE STUDY: NOVERO

Innovation creates new refined markets. A case in point is a German company. novero (its name and logo are intentionally written in lower case). Along with supplying Bluetooth/wireless solutions to automotive manufacturers such as Jaguar, Land Rover and BMW, its mission is to cater to a niche consumer market by creating lifestyle accessories that build unique levels of loyalty among sophisticated end-users rather than simply create an affordable line of "me-too"/traditional wireless phone headsets.

To that end, the company launched exquisite *Bluetooth* communication pieces, for use with mobile phones, which are worn around the neck when not in use. Designs include a necklace with Lapis lazuli set with sterling silver and another with genuine pearls and gold. As expected, they are available only at select retailers in North America, Europe and Asia.

Novero knew from the outset that its unique and pricey jewelry would not be for everyone but it suits them well. Their niche products fall under the premium/luxury sector, which is intended for the gadget-admiring "Fashionistas" and discerning consumers who also own fine watches and possibly a top luxury mobile phone such as "Vertu" or "Tag Heur."

THE "IDEAL" NICHE PLAYER

A niche market player is very effective at working closely with customers to build and maintain long term relationships by innovating and challenging the existing norms in the industry, thus adding value to the project, program, and organizational level. If one is considered an expert in what one does by focusing in one area, then great success will follow. The value proposition must be relevant to the target market. This means a target market must be clearly defined. Focusing on a specific market requires knowing it inside and out. This includes conducting a market analysis, stating a precise target market description and goal, as well as being clear about the type of relationship one would like to achieve with his/her market.

By definition, then, a business which focuses on a niche market is supplying a need for a product or service that is not being met by mainstream providers. As such, one can think of a niche market as a narrowly defined group of potential clients offering them the best of what you have. In return, their vendors will profit from higher margins and customer loyalty. As for targeting smaller "sub" niches, you will find them much easier to dominate.

"Experience marketing defines the future of marketing. We live in an increasingly consumer controlled marketplace — from the way people personalize the music they'll listen to, the type of news they want to receive and the delivery system that brings them that news. The only way to maintain an adequate degree of relevance as a marketer is to provide the consumer an experience in the self-defined and controlled sphere in which he lives."

-**Erik Hauser**

Demonstrate Rather than Tell: How Experiential Marketing is Creating a Sea-Change in the World of Branding and Advertising

Ask any consumer what they think of all the advertising messages they are exposed to on a daily basis and chances are the majority, as most surveys have revealed, believe there is far too much advertising noise — whether offline or online. A sizable percentage of consumers have also admitted that they avoid purchasing products that over-advertise.

Several months ago, I attended a local conference organized by a Canadian marketing group. I was drawn to one of the key-note speakers in particular who made a compelling presentation on the benefits of "experiential marketing." To me this clever approach was the antithesis to traditional advertising which is generally a monologue. Rather than sell the features of products or services, you apply innovation to draw your ad audience's full attention to your wares. What's more, this tactic builds brand awareness which settles longer in the mind of the consumer — allowing people to experience the benefits for themselves. As consumers are bombarded with multiple messages daily, companies ought to find a way to keep their brands top-of-mind and earn loyalty.

The speaker I was referring to here is Max Lenderman — a pioneer in the field of experiential marketing who is also an award-winning published author, a sought-after speaker and media commentator on this subject. Lenderman encourages businesses to look beyond traditional communication to get customers interacting with and living their brands. He frequently utilizes the expression/slogan, "Experience the message".

EXPERIENTIAL BRANDING VS. EXPERIENTIAL MARKETING

Experiential branding refers to differentiating a product or service in the consumers' mind by focusing on the total experience, rather than focusing on the features, benefits or attributes of the product, whereas, *experiential marketing* signifies integrating brand or product messages into consumers' lives in the form of interactive experiences, rather than delivering them through traditional static media such as television or in print.

IN TODAY'S ECONOMY: BUYING EXPERIENCES AND CONVERSATIONS

Experience-based marketing tactics which fall under the category of "guerilla marketing," are consumer-centric. The approach gives customers an opportunity to engage and interact with products and services in creative and compelling ways. The goal is to establish the connection in a way that the consumer responds to a product offering built upon emotional and rational response levels. The unique experience can turn viral as word will spread quickly to others. Therefore, the aim of the experiential marketer is to add excitement with a dose of entertainment to what otherwise might pass as lackluster.

Marketing guru Philip Kotler, in his book "*Marketing insights from A to Z: 80 concepts every manager needs to know*", states that marketing *experiences* or designing experiences around goods and services have many illustrations. For example, great restaurants are known for their experience as much as their food. Starbucks charges $2 or more to experience coffee at its finest. Restaurants such as Planet Hollywood and Hard Rock Café are specifically set up as an experience. Las Vegas hotels, anxious to distinguish themselves, take on the character of ancient Rome or New York City. But the master was Walt Disney, who created the opportunity to experience the cowboy West, fairyland castles, pirate ships, and the like.

Those who follow Apple know that their Genius Bar is a huge success. The concept offers its customers:

- Free advice,

- A well designed ambiance;

- Well-trained and friendly staff;

- Appointments that can be set to avoid long waiting periods.

With the Genius Bar, Apple created a conversation. When you enter their stores, you experience a two-way conversation along with your expectations being met or exceeded.

LOYALTY LESSONS: CASE STUDIES OF EFFECTIVE EXPERIENTIAL CAMPAIGNS

P&G's Tide — CleanStart mobile free laundry service

Tide CleanStart first launched in the wake of Hurricane Katrina in 2005 to provide clean clothes for affected families in New Orleans. The resilience and spirit of the people of New Orleans inspired Tide to expand the program and bring the laundry service to Southern California, helping families affected by the wildfires of October 2007. Collectively, Tide has washed more than 30,000 loads of laundry for New Orleans and Southern California families. The Tide CleanStart truck is now prepared to help displaced residents, people in shelters and other people whose homes and personal items have been impacted by the Iowa flood.

Times Square and Toilet Paper
As posted by Jill Griffin in customerthink.com (Jan 23, 2008).
Toilet Paper. How do you successfully build an engaging, loyalty-building brand story around *that* product? Just ask the ace marketers at Proctor & Gamble and they'll likely tell you about the 20 free, deluxe Charmin restrooms opened in New York's Time Square for the 2007 holiday season. At the same location in 2006, the Charmin Holiday rest rooms served more than 420,000 people from 100 countries and all 50 states, so a 2007 encore was in order.

But free, family-friendly restrooms and ample toilet tissue were just one part of the unique, memorable brand story crafted by the Charmin team. First, friendly folks dressed as dancing toilets greeted passersby on the street, inviting them to visit the Charmin Holiday Restrooms nearby. Visitors then took escalators up and wove through a rope line while a legion of smiling hosts wearing Charmin apparel greeted them and upbeat holiday music played in the background. Inside the stalls (serviced by staff after every use), Ultra Strong and Ultra Soft tissue were available and afterwards, guests were asked to vote for their favorite.

MAKING IT WORK

Experiential marketing should strive to:

- Deliver a meaningful benefit to the consumer;
- Engage people in a memorable ways;
- Be authentic;
- Deliver relevant communication to consumers only where and when they are most responsive to them;
- Succeed using innovation to reach consumers in creative and compelling ways.

TODAY'S ACTIONABLE INSIGHT

Whether it's online or in the field, you should start a conversation with your customers. All merchants offer products and/or services. However, don't simply view a transaction as a transaction and time to move on to the next. That is getting rarer. The challenge is to usher your customer through a memorable experience that will yield long-term benefits for the client and your business.

"If you don't get noticed, you don't have anything. You just have to be noticed, but the art is in getting noticed naturally, without screaming or without tricks."

– Leo Burnett

Ambiance Marketing: A Multi-Sensory Approach to Attracting and Retaining Clientele

The dictionary describes "ambiance" as "the character and feeling of a place." A place which wants to attract the most discerning souls should be unique and embody a complete lifestyle concept which combines a relaxed, spiritual ambiance in an elegant setting and decor with attention to detail. Staging an impressive, well-executed upscale event, such as a product launch or promotion takes creativity, organizational skills, as well as savoir faire.

Pleasing hors d'oeuvres and drinks prepared and presented with pizzazz are complemented by soothing music which is also an integral part of the ambience and ranges from classic music to smooth jazz or chill-out rhythms. The attractive, smiling and well mannered staff are dressed stylishly.

All of these elements combined will, undoubtedly, seduce the senses and generate good vibes and create positive memories. This principle applies equally well to business establishments and brands and includes boutique hotels, restaurants and bars, fashion boutiques and other upscale business establishments. In marketing, a multi-sensory approach is proven to increase sales.

To be effective, the use of an integrated approach is essential across various touch points with the purpose of engaging customers. This is accomplished by connecting the emotions to a product or service, and infusing it with a tangible and intangible essence that remain in the customers' minds.

The ambiance you create is one of your best marketing tools. The aesthetic appeal to the human senses, the feel of your business and the brand you create is your image. Along with great service, it is one of the most important reasons customers will choose you over the competition.

WHAT SHOULD YOU CONSIDER WHEN DEVELOPING AMBIANCE?

In keeping with the spirit of our five senses, you can exploit them entirely to create a favorable experience in synergy, for guests and clients alike. Below are some of the most important factors:

Sight: choice of lighting, décor, colors and an ergonomic layout. You can get a real sense of movement using these elements. Lighting is also very helpful when it comes to the overall event. Low intensity lighting such as dimmed soft halogen or LED lights along with the presence of lit candles create a stress-free atmosphere. In addition to your building materials and lighting, the art you choose to put on your walls will make a huge impact on the overall ambiance.

Local art, modern art, renaissance art or a hodgepodge of all of them will help convey the ambiance you are trying to define.

Listen: music, effects, volume and vibrations. The tone and the energy of the room can be set with the right music selections. Think about using a "signature" sound effect to draw attention to different happenings throughout establishment or event.

Upbeat music that would be appropriate in the evening may not appeal to your morning customers who have just gotten out of bed. If you have an Italian-themed bar, you may want to interject some Italian music from artists like Zucchero or Eros Ramazotti. If your theme/branding and ambiance is geared to a very hip, young audience, it will likely suit your customers to include songs with a driving beat from cutting-edge alternative and electronic artists.

Touch: textures and comfort. This is all about how your guests and/or clients interact with the environment. Plenty of emphasis should be placed on this when designing the layout. It should be ergonomic. The more comfortable the space, the longer guests/clients will linger in any given area.

The materials you use to build out your operation will be a major component of the ambiance of your business and the choices are many. Countertops can be granite, frosted glass, laminate or of exotic wood. Floors can range from acid-etched concrete to terrazzo to granite. The use of wood can evoke a feeling of warmth. Exposed pipes and air ducts can give your business an industrial feel. Draperies can dampen sound and add texture.

Taste: finding the perfect balance between sour, salty, sweet, and bitter during menu designs and beverage selections with the intention of pleasing most taste buds. Presentation is equally important which has an impact on the overall image of the setting.

Smell: it is all about fragrance which aids in creating emotion. This sense is usually neglected yet of all our senses, the sense of smell is closely linked to emotion and memory. You can use something as simple as burning incense or candles to something far more complex like computer controlled scent machines to enhance your environment.

This could just be the icing on the cake, sort of speak, in complementing the overall mood. If it is a French bakery café style of operation, the smell of roasted coffee and baked items sold will induce clients to make and increase their purchases.

A case in point in terms of a successful establishment that, implemented the above principles spot on, is a popular upscale "member's only" bar in Dallas, Texas called *Candleroom*. It did not become renowned simply by accident.

This has been accomplished by developing and executing the perfect atmosphere for young professionals seeking to socialize in a dramatic and spacious setting — a progressive urban lounge modern in design and decorated with bold, sensuous colors. The ultra swanky décor with its velvet, leather and fine furniture are lit by candles and dimmed chandeliers.

DJs spin house, rock, hip-hop and dance for those that are interested in a little more of a dance club setting, while the attractive staff working behind the bars mix exotic drinks for the patrons. As a result, it is considered by many discerning clubbers to be one of the most handsome drinking destinations in Dallas.

FOCUS GROUPS: UNCOVERING YOUR CUSTOMERS' SPECIFIC DESIRES FOR YOUR SUCCESS

As companies grow larger, they commonly hire a market research firm to determine what their customers like, dislike and what additional products or services they desire. This is often uncovered through the use of focus groups.

There is no reason you cannot poll customers in your area in the same way large multinational companies do with great success. Focus groups can be helpful if you are already open or just beginning to plan your business. Rather than simply assuming, it is in your best interest to know if you are giving your customers the products, services and ambiance they desire.

Feedback is important, hence you need to find out what your customers' needs are and fulfill as many of them as possible. After you analyze the information you have received from your focus group, try to incorporate the best and most workable ideas into a motif that will define your business and create the ideal ambiance to attract and keep your customers.

ON A SIDE NOTE: BRANDED CD COMPILATION

Designing and implementing custom music and visual strategies that emotionally anchor a brand to its clients, should be considered. The goal of branded CDs is to turn your listeners into disciples of your brand. Every aspect of your custom CD says something about your brand, therefore, custom CD's place equal importance on print, media, and visual elements in addition to the music.

Specialty music compilation companies such as Sonodea and Custom CD Corporation oversee all logistics related to custom branded CD music compilation and development. They work closely with clients on everything from the music themes to the packaging to the visual content. This ensures that the music, look and feel of the CD resonate with their customers' clientele and target demographic.

In some ways, all business is show-business and storytelling. Brand image is all about the experience, perception and differentiation you create in the customers' mind.

Ambiance marketing takes all this into meaningful consideration by applying its multi-sensory approach to attracting and retaining clientele to your brand and business establishment.

"**Effective communication is 20% what you know and 80% how you feel about what you know.**"

— Jim Rohn

Marketing Strategy vs. Public Relations — In Tune with The Times

There is a fallacy that most public relations firms do PR. Essentially they do publicity. How's that possible, you ask? Well, this is according to marketing gurus and what's stated in Wikipedia:

"Public relations and publicity are not synonymous but many PR campaigns include provisions for publicity. Publicity is the spreading of information to gain public awareness for a product, person, service, cause or organization, and can be seen as a result of effective PR planning."

PR, then, is the creative strategy of a story. It's focused on its intended audience and with the full utilization of the tools at its disposal, such as press releases, speeches, online social media and public service activities amongst others, can determine what and how people talk about a company, a brand, a product. With the emergence of the Web 2.0 networks and technologies, viral videos have engendered the new online marketing concept which is Viral Video Marketing. It is usually shared over blogs, email or instant messages and other media-sharing websites.

Steve Jobs and the initial iPad successfully got placed on the cover of more than 60 magazines in the year the product launched. That's referred to as "publicity." However, the real challenge was crafting the storyline of the highly sought after iPad — along with the story of Steve Jobs. That's PR work at its finest.

PRESS RELEASES IN TUNE WITH THE TIMES

The words "Press Release" or "Press Statement" go back a long while when such written communication were printed and released to the press to spread the noteworthy news. These days the more common term used is "News Release" since it has a broader meaning. Materials are now posted online, either via newswire services, within a company and to other non-paid and to some extent, paid sources. As for the term "Media Release", it's like a brief newspaper article that is sent to media outlets to gain their interest and if they accept it, they will then publish a story about it.

DEMYSTIFYING THE ROLES OF PR AND MARKETING

In the same way that PR and Publicity are not equal, the same goes for the former and marketing. Marketing is interested in the understanding of the consumer to meet his/her needs/desires, the goals of the company and to help the company find a way to profitably meet those needs. Public relations, on the other hand, works to build relationships with various sources, reduce conflict and improve cooperation between a company and its intended audience. Marketing focuses on selling and packaging products or services, whereas, public relations is more about reputation, crisis and image management as well as brand building. As the renowned marketing strategist Al Ries succinctly stated, "PR builds brands. Advertising maintains brands once they are built by PR." Clever public relations will undoubtedly create a healthy environment for marketing. This requires a team with innovative minds.

Marketing and PR, therefore work best when they are treated as separate organizational functions. Nonetheless, they must coordinate in a team effort to make certain they are working to achieve the same objectives. Advertising is an effective marketing tool and is frequently used in conjunction with PR, sales promotion and personal selling strategies in a marketing mix. Advertising is good at building brand awareness for a large general audience, while PR works for communicating to a more select audience. Hence, advertising usually emphasizes the credentials, roots and legitimacy, bringing assurance, while public relations reinforce the excitement, the risk and emotions.

IT'S THE IMAGE, SILLY!

Any seasoned PR practitioner will tell you that a favorable corporate reputation and image are an essential part of their mission whether it's to retain, recapture their clients' esteem or to promote a favorable impression for a public company's existing and potential investors. However, companies should also be proactive and focus on their behavior instead of on words alone. As for brand building and awareness, a PR firm can implement a great brand story and distribute it through the appropriate target media which will be perceived as authentic and unbiased as opposed to a paid advertisement.

To retain the shine on one's brand assets, companies are encouraged to frequent online chatter where people exchange gossip and views. Prevention is undoubtedly better than cure. By spotting problems early you could seize on an impasse before it spreads further and tarnishes your reputation.

SURVEY SAYS!

To offer a noteworthy rationale for media exposure, depending on the industry one's in, companies should consider hiring a polling firm to conduct a survey about some worthwhile trend which is relevant to their product or service and which would be of interest to the general public or a niche market. The results from the credible poll can be used as an ideal story line for the media. A case in point is Berlitz Canada which carried-out a poll, through Harris/Decima during several days in March 2008, via an online panel, sampling 1,277 adult Canadians about the benefits of being bilingual or multilingual — especially with regards to career advancement opportunities. The results were exploited by being turned into a publicity feat which formed additional exposure Berlitz wouldn't have otherwise received in the traditional sense.

CUSTOMER CARE IN AN IDEAL WORLD

What is the meaning of paying a PR firm to glorify your reputation along with your product or service if you can't deliver on your promises? Today's consumer is not simply sophisticated but with swift access to the Internet he/she can vent their frustration online through Twitter, blogs and plenty more social media sources. Much is touted by companies about customer service/relations but surprisingly only a few actually deliver on their promises. At the outset, it appears that many lack a vital customer relations policy including inadequate staff training and coaching. Consider hiring a mystery shopper service to gauge your service performance and make any necessary improvements.

WHAT'S NEXT? PR, THE NEW MEDIA AND TALENT FOR HIRE

Over the years, clients have become more demanding of their service providers. They have come to expect more personalized interaction, customized solutions, timely results and most certainly a "bang for their buck." PR firms are expected to be more transparent, specialized in particular fields, rather than general practitioners, and embrace the de-facto new media sources — the online social media which is nowadays being integrated with PR. This includes blogging, Twittering, social networking and viral marketing amongst others. That is to say, be in the forefront of new fields of media and communication which will be fully utilized in the business of influencing perceptions.

In addition, one other notable trend is towards widespread audio and video production and communication. From podcasting to mobile video, audio and video will predominate in our world. PR has traditionally been all about effective written communications. While that will remain important, the new skills required to be part of a society driven by other media forms will be critical. With the plethora of multinational and boutique PR firms out there, differentiation in the delivery of services, personalized service and focus in niche markets/industries will be the determining core value equation.

Hiring the right practitioners should include candidates with a variety of business experience especially in marketing and negotiations including strong written communications. Additionally, prospective PR practitioners should possess soft skills, common sense, and flair to think laterally and be someone who gets excited by ideas. A communications or marketing degree should be considered an asset rather than a pre-requisite.

PR practitioners need more skills today than at any time in the past because there are more tasks, more media and more tools. Hence, a comprehensive in-house training program, as well as outside educational encouragement and support, should be part of a firm's perquisites to their staff. The fact of the matter is, companies that invest in their employees' education and training receive loyalty and better results from them.

"I am not looking like Armani today and somebody else tomorrow. I look like Ralph Lauren. And my goal is to constantly move in fashion and move in style without giving up what I am."

— **Ralph Lauren**

Lifestyle Branding: Engagement and Total Experience

When you visit your local Porsche dealership be prepared to engage. Staff will talk to you about the total experience. This will invariably include discussing the firm's racing pedigree and performance. In your mind, you will be able to feel the steering wheel, smell the leather seats, and hear the roar of the engine. This car represents to you an exclusive club and you desire to be part of the privileged few. Clearly, one does not buy a Porsche simply to go from point A to point B. In practice, you might use this care to commute to work, but this is not the incentive to purchase a piece of automobile and racing history.

Porsche is clearly a brand with authenticity and heritage. The principles shaping the consumer's buying behavior go beyond intention. There is a sense of engagement in fulfilling a dream. It can be to make a social status statement or a personal style choice. Whatever it is, it is not an unconscious choice. The codifiers are clear: This is who I am, and what I believe in. Ultimately, it can also articulate your sense of self-worth and your emotional aspirations.

The most important emotional benefit in my view is that a product of this caliber and class expresses itself when the consumer can declare, "It suits my lifestyle."

LIFESTYLE BRANDS MATTER

Not every brand is a lifestyle brand regardless of whether it strives to portray itself as such. A company can define itself as a lifestyle brand when its products promote more than a product with key benefits and attributes. Note however that lifestyle branding is more than just promoting "a way of life". It is a product or service that provides consumers with an emotional attachment to the lifestyle of the brand. Think of Ralph Lauren and you can readily see it is not about the clothes. It becomes an attachment like Porsche to an exclusive club in which you can be a member through emotional identification through use of the products in question.

Smart companies understand these principles and look to keep the customer engaged. By doing so, they clearly forge the sort of long term relationships, which become the envy of their designated sector. Financial benefits clearly follow, but the raison d'être of the firm must back up its promotion for this to work effectively. One reason so many firms want to enter the lifestyle arena is profitability and high profit margins. Established brands can tap economies of scale when they launch new products at a cheaper cost to the firm. Surplus revenue can then be channeled into extensive advertising and promotion costs.

BUILDING A LIFESTYLE BRAND

Generally speaking, a brand that is designed for the lifestyle segment should have more emotional value to consumers. Features, cost, and benefits do play a role but by themselves they would be insignificant.

There are companies that become a lifestyle brand by tying their product ranges to a distinctive culture or group. Marketing guru, Seth Godin labels this with the key word as a "tribe". A classic case is Harley Davidson, who sells branded merchandise to customers whether or not they own one of the firm's motorcycles. Calvin Klein has also done this by licensing its name to the perfume line called EUPHORIA. Other key lifestyle brands include Hackett, Hermes, Louis Vuitton and the Abercrombie & Fitch phenomenon.

In the electronics and computer industries, it is uncommon to have lifestyle products. However, Apple has broken this "glass ceiling" by its unconventionality with iPod, iPhone and its online music store. Even its ubiquitous white headphones have become a fashion accessory and, some would even argue, a status symbol. The people who follow Apple and its "lifestyle" are clearly all obsessed in a way that the firm intended when it embarked on this well-thought-through strategy.

Lifestyle brands have clearly impacted on luxury brand management. The usual suspects such as BMW, Armani, W Hotels, and Rolex — just to name a few, have fostered commitment and loyalty with their promotional campaigns. These have given consumers an "associate" status with all that is glamorous. Just think of Daniel Craig and James Bond. Sales at Omega thrive on this "Bond engagement".

The methods to reach a target audience require an integrated marketing/communication strategy. They clearly require taking into consideration and harmonizing the following aspects:

- Experiential Marketing;
- Grassroots marketing;
- Promotional tours;
- Sponsorship of lifestyle events;
- Lifestyle marketing on the Web: think Facebook;
- Viral video marketing;
- Social media/networking (blogs, chat rooms & message boards);
- "Interactive" is key;
- Mobile phone media, text messaging & applications.

NOT EVERY BRAND CAN BE A "LIFESTYLE"

New research from Kellogg at Northwestern finds that the strategy of traditional brands to reposition themselves as a "lifestyle" brand may fail. The reason is not rocket science: they simply fail to "bond" with their customer base.

"The open vistas of lifestyle branding are an illusion," said Alexander Chernev, lead author of the study and Associate Professor of Marketing at Kellogg. "By switching to lifestyle positioning, brands might be trading the traditional in-category competition for even fiercer cross-category competition. Now they have to compete not only with their direct rivals but also with brands from unrelated categories. Focusing on lifestyle puts brands like Gillette, Abercrombie & Fitch, Harley-Davidson, Starbucks, Apple, and Facebook in direct competition with one another."

The study reveals how brands serve as a means of self-expression along with the limitations of expressing a consumer's identity through brands. Moreover, the study uncovers customers' desire for self-expression through brands is finite.

IN PERSPECTIVE

Forward-thinking brands are those which will continue to develop creative ideas and solutions that will allow people to interact with each other and explore, as well as share creative opportunities. Moreover, those same brands will make it a strategic priority to add pleasure into the lives of their consumers.

To be sure, there are many excellent examples of lifestyle branding. Just examine the "hotel as lifestyle" creator, Ian Schrager. Since the 1970's, as an entrepreneur, Chairman and Chief Executive Officer of Ian Schrager Company, he has achieved international recognition for concepts that have revolutionized both the entertainment and hospitality industries.

His passionate commitment to the modern lifestyle has been expressed through a series of pioneering concepts:

The hotel is no longer just a place to sleep. It is portrayed as your home away from home. This allows hotels to act like theater. Think of the boutique hotel or "cheap chic", "lobby socializing", the resort, or the spa.

His keen instincts for the mood and feel of popular culture were honed during the 1970s and 1980s, when he and his late business partner, Steve Rubell, created Studio 54 and Palladium. In 1984, they turned their attention to Morgan's Hotel and introduced the concept of "boutique hotel" to the world, which is today one the hottest segments in hospitality.

The goal of a lifestyle brand is to get people to relate to one another through a "concept brand." These brands successfully sell identity, image and status rather than a "product-service" in the traditional meaning of the term.

If they are successful in capturing their audience, then they become legends in their own right. If you examine the recently published photographic testament to "*Il Pelicano*" in Tuscany you will understand perfectly the meaning of the lifestyle branding spirit.

"The source of the water provides a good foundation for differentiation,"

— Rob Frankel, *Branding Consultant*

Branding Bottled Water: Differentiating a Commodity Through Various Tactics

Make no mistake bottled water is a billion dollar business. All the major food and drinks groups are involved. Branding drives this market whether it is Poland Springs, Fiji water, and that trendy water of choice on the Left Bank of Paris, St. George from Corsica with its striking design bottle by the French designer, Philippe Starck.

The reasons driving the market are changes in lifestyle, attitudes towards drinks in general, and the simple fact that water is the proverbial "elixir" of life. Remember the simple fact that our bodies are made-up of 60-70% water.

Doctors recommend an average daily intake of H2O should be 8-12 eight-ounce glasses, daily. As a "commodity", 7.56 liters/256 U.S. fluid ounces are consumed daily by an "average" household. Although prices vary according to brand, the average liter/fl. oz. price tag is equivalent to a liter/fl. oz. of petrol in Canada.

Another remarkable fact is that in the 1990s, Perrier through its clever and witty advertising campaigns worldwide made water the chic and socially acceptable drink of preference at parties and social occasions. You were now no longer forced to imbibe alcohol at a "business" lunch as a meeting to seal a deal unless you wanted to.

FEATURES OF THE AMERICAN MARKET

Although many Americans drink tap water, the consumption of bottled water was estimated to have risen in 2010 to about 9.4 million gallons (35.5m liters). This is the rough equivalent of $16.8 billion in turnover of bottled water sales.

These astonishing figures demonstrate the value of water in monetary terms and show why over the last 10 years food and drinks groups have pursued an aggressive acquisition strategy in snatching up once independent brands. Although there are many global players, the market has also seen the emergence of a core of key groups with their ever-growing portfolios of brands, each distinct and recognizable in the marketplace. Brands are for both the sparkling and still/ spring water segments.

If you combine the fact that branding can be executed with vending machines a la Coca-Cola at the entry price of $150k, you can understand the attractiveness.

Walk down the drinks aisle in any American supermarket for example and you will be simply amazed by the vast choices confronting customers.

TOP PLAYERS

Examining this market more closely, you will discover that two principal firms dominate the branded water market in developed markets. I will not address the interests of Coca-Cola and the PepsiCo group here, nor their activities in Asia, particularly India. Although this is another fascinating study on branding and the bottled purified water market.

Looking more closely, the two firms, that stand out are Groupe Danone (Paris) and Nestle (Vaud). The Danone portfolio consists of many recognizable names such as Evian, Volvic, Badoit and in North America, Dannon Spring Water.

Nestle on the other hand, holds Vittel, Poland Springs, Deer Park and in the sparkling category, Perrier and San Pellegrino.

Currently, the number one selling premium brand of still water in terms of volume is Evian; the brand is recognized for its pedigree, coming from the Alps and its purity.

WATER CATEGORIES

Experts break the bottled water market into two constituent groups: non-carbonated water and carbonated water. Non-carbonated water is often called "mineral" water and can be designated be distilled, filtered, spring or well.

Sparkling water is identified by naturally occurring carbonation or water, which has been injected with carbonization.

A third category of water is "fancy" or value-added water. Two brands, which stick out are "Clearly Canadian" and Vitamin Water". Both lines propose enhance products that can include flavoring and/or vitamins. The last few years has seen an explosion of vitamin water. Certain critics see vitamin water as mere marketing hype. Others believe that it has carved out a vital and important niche by adding a new product range to a market concerned with "health" attributes.

How can one differentiate and command a premium price for water?

Drinks groups have successfully proved that with creativity and a compelling storyline, just about anything can be branded successfully, including commodities. Since selling water is not about technological dominance, the key discriminator is "brand" and "brand identity." The other key factor in the mix is logistics and distribution. Both are essential elements to high sales figures.

"If there weren't any branding in the water category, the business would eventually go 100% to price and to private label," says Robert Lynn, Executive Vice-President of Sales and Marketing for Global Beverage Systems, marketers of Le Nature's Beverages.

For the moment, he is convinced that brand is more important than price.

APPROACHES TO PRODUCT DIFFERENTIATION

The most common approaches to differentiating water that the marketing professionals apply are:

- Fancy bottle and label packaging: the bottle shape, color/ codes and functionality really do matter;

- The actual "Source" and promotional "story", highlighting uniqueness;

- Health qualities that promote fitness and well-being;

- Flavor enhancements: This can include orange, lemon and lime. It is also an excellent and healthy soda substitute;

- Lifestyle;

- Adding unusual and compact/practical sizes: think bicycle bottles with nozzle;

- Limited price offers or bundling with other products;

- Solid and extensive distribution channel with retailers and institutional clients;

- Sponsorships for additional exposure and significant opportunities for distinct marketing.

THE BOTTLED WATER MYTH

Many people perceive bottled water as the "picture" of purity. Think of the label used by Evian and its snow capped Alps. However, tap water is actually subject to stricter (U.S., Canadian and European) government standards throughout most municipalities, especially large cities. Bacteria testing are stricter than is required for bottled water.

"There's no guarantee that bottled water is any safer than the water that comes out of your tap," says Wendy Gordon of the non-profit Natural Resources Defence Council. In fact, 25% of bottled water comes from municipalities own water sources. Research into 28 mineral and spring waters published in 1995 found that all had what the regulations defined as a low mineral content. You really cannot rely on these waters to make a significant contribution to your mineral intake, the report concluded.

ENVIRONMENTALISTS SCORN BOTTLED WATER, EMBRACE REFILLABLE CONTAINERS

What makes the bottled water labels marketing more challenging these days is the bad press and pressure they're getting from the Green movement.

"It's a ridiculous waste," said Eric Yverbaum, co-founder of the Tappening.com campaign he started with his friend Mark Di Massimo to educate the public about what it takes to produce plastic containers that take hundreds of years to break down in landfills. Because of this, environmental activists and a growing number of restaurants are propagating a pro-tap water movement.

That's good news for Brita, the world's leading manufacturer of filter systems for tap water. Its products come in two forms: faucet mounts or pitchers. On their website, they claim to transform your regular tap water into a source that makes you feel more alive. Is it any wonder, then, that this company is becoming a noteworthy competitor to the water bottling companies?

Today, only about 20% of plastic water bottles are being recycled, which is startling when you consider that over 35 billion plastic bottles of water are sold in the U.S. alone each year. As a result, municipalities such as Toronto — one of the biggest cities in the world — to have banned bottled water. Montreal's ban will go into effect in 2015. Watch for other cities worldwide to follow suit. Innovative individuals/companies have found a solution to this. Thanks to them, the next disposable alternative to bottled water has already hit our shelves in the form of boxed water. As of this writing, there are five such companies (H2O Pure Spring Water, O.N.E. Water, Aqua2Go, Boxed Water Is Better and ICEBOX) producing and selling boxed water — mainly through the use of Sweden's well known milk and juice carton packaging manufacturer, TetraPak.

The 360 Paper Bottle is the first of its kind in the world, and an eco-friendly solution to the problem of plastic water bottles. About 90% of the boxed water container is made from a renewable resource. H2O Natural Spring Water, which gets its source from the underground aquifer at the renowned Niagara Falls region in Canada, is a sustainable option for "water on the go". Those bottles are made mainly of paper, a sustainable and renewable resource, from responsibly sourced, well managed forests where new trees replace harvested ones. So far, these companies have been well-received by eco-concerned consumers/devotees.

WATER AS THE ULTIMATE LUXURY

How about branding water and putting the world's most expensive price tag on it?

That's just what its founder and president, Kevin G. Boyd, did for Bling H2O, which he labels as a "luxury" product. He charges on average $44 per bottle. This has been accomplished through a clever marketing strategy, emphasizing:

1. Focusing on the distribution of limited editions;

2. Creating a fancy glass water bottle to add a "chic" cachet;

3. Conveying a glamorous storyline with a special focus on celebrity status, using personalities to represent the brand.

For example, Kevin Boyd recently introduced the Dubai Collection's "The Ten Thousand" with a price tag of $2,600 per bottle. This bottle has over 10,000 hand-applied Swarovski Crystals with each bottle custom made to order, numbered and comes with a pair of white handling gloves and an attractive case.

I cannot imagine anyone paying for this. However, he has proved there is a market, although a microscopic niche.

MARKET EVOLUTION

It is clear that the bottled water market will continue to expand. At the global level sales already top $35bn. The key for the firms involved will be differentiation, added or perceived added value, packaging and innovation. Grabbing the customers' attention is the name of the game.

What you can conclude is that this humble commodity most of us take for granted is no longer so humble.

"The aim of marketing is to know and understand the customer so well the product or service fits him and sells itself."

— Peter Drucker

Post Recession Marketing Approach: Adapting the Message to a Changing Consumer

To say the global recession was a wake-up call for the most consumers would be quite an understatement. It is just one of many events that have weakened people's sense of security in the past decade along with political instability, terrorism and environmental issues such as global warming were already significant even before financial markets collapsed. As a result, there has been a mood of mistrust and anxiety that developed among many people around the world, which has produced a reexamination of priorities and values.

A recent study from Ogilvy & Mather in the U.S. identified new consumer priorities with quality of life and peace of mind at the top — and a focus on living life in a more sustainable way from both an environmental and financial point of view.

MARKETERS TO RESPOND TO SHIFT IN CONSUMER BEHAVIOR

A paradigm shift is required to deal with a new, more conscious consumer and to design strategies that will pertain to such a shift in behavior and thinking. Consumers are buying fewer products, fewer brands, and being more careful in their choices. In general, people are relying less on brands for fulfillment or status and are now considering other values and priorities into their choices.

Some experts think that when the recession is over, consumers will return to their spendthrift ways. However, this time that behavior may not hold true. Predictions and surveys abound that the post-recession consumer will be different. Although he/she may have been forced by circumstances to reassess their spending habits, many consumers have found that spending prudently equates to good value for money.

Data from a variety of sources support this view. A recently released survey by the Pew Research Center in the United States reported that 71% of Americans said they have switched to less expensive brands as a result of the recession. Also in the United States, a study by Deloitte found that 84% of shoppers were examining their grocery purchases, looking for ways to save money. Seventy-nine percent said that they were "smarter" shoppers than they were two years earlier, and nearly the same proportion (75 percent) said that the need to reduce spending had made them understand which brands were really important to them. A Sanford C. Bernstein survey conducted in December 2009 found that half of consumers had not only traded down to less expensive products but found them to be "as good or better than" the costlier brands they replaced.

WHAT DOES THIS SIGNIFY FOR THE NEW APPROACHES TO MARKETING?

Uncertainty equals opportunity. This is a time of great opportunity for businesses if they take the long view — especially with their marketing activities. While consumer priorities have changed, the basic challenge for advertisers is the same — to deliver a pertinent message in creative ways. This can be accomplished by utilizing new approaches and making their communications relevant to the current concerns of the "new" consumers, who are now selecting brands for different purposes compared to pre-recessionary times. Today, brands need to create strategies to address consumer transformations. They should position themselves in line with contemporary consumer needs, as well as against their competing brands. The approaches will differ according to the product category and the market segment within that category, but a few highly successful global brands are already showing the way. Marketers should take notice from these examples.

A premium brand that is thriving in the new age of consumerism is Nespresso. The company has succeeded in defining itself as a "new luxury brand." Even during a period of relative modesty in spending, people are not willing to live without a few luxuries. Nespresso has tapped into people's desire to indulge them by offering them the same high-quality drink brewed at home. Plenty of marketing spending was accomplished a few years back to support the premium positioning of the brand. To demonstrate the attraction of Nespresso coffee, its ad agency created stories in which the actor George Clooney goes unrecognized and unnoticed in Nespresso stores. Clearly, the message that was conveyed was that the coffee is what is important to the clientele, rather than the endorsement of a celebrity.

In the personal care category, Unilever's Dove brand has been taking aim at traditional standards of beauty, by means of the "Campaign for Real Beauty", as well as viral videos such as "Onslaught". By having focused on this creative direction, Dove has redirected the debate on beauty and scored a unique category for itself.

Another example of a brand that has benefited from people's need to seek new and less costly ways to achieve satisfaction is McDonald's. The recent campaign in France, called, "Come as You Are", is based on the idea that there are not enough places where we can go to truly relax and be ourselves. This campaign, which generated a great deal of attention, showed the different personalities of McDonald's customers. The message: "You not only get good food at a reasonable price, but you can eat what you like, stay as long as you wish, and simply be yourself."

THE CONSCIOUS POST-RECESSION CONSUMER AND NEW MARKETING TACTICS

Conscious and mindful consumption does not always translate to purchasing less. It means that consumers will reconsider and focus their spending money on the most psychologically rewarding purchases. During the recession, such purchases will almost certainly offer the benefit of security, whereas in post-recession, they're more likely to be focused on products that bring vitality and sensation to life, offer opportunities for self-expression and personal development and are environmentally friendly.

How companies reshape their marketing strategy going forward will depend a lot on who their customers are. However, what all consumers will have in common is a strong focus on price. Another suggestion is to be visible when customers are ready to purchase what you offer both offline and online. Regardless of gender and across almost every income level, one thing is clear, the recession has shaken the status quo for consumers and it seems as if the trend will be irreversible.

"You'll never have a product or price advantage again. They can be easily duplicated, but a strong customer service culture can't be copied."

— Jerry Fritz

Chapter V: Customer Engagement

The Customer Experience: Building a Customer-Centric Organization

It doesn't take a genius to realize how few companies these days actually "Walk the talk." What does this mean, you ask? I refer to "the total customer experience".

Richard Owen, Vice President of Dell online worldwide, says,

"It's the sum total of the interactions that a customer has with a company's products, people, and processes. It goes from the moment when customers see an advert to the moment when they accept delivery of a product and beyond.

Sure, we want people to think that our computers are great. However, what matters is the totality of customers' experiences with us: talking with our call-center representatives, visiting our Web site, buying a PC, and owning a PC. The customer experience reflects all of those interactions."

You can claim that Richard Owen *would* say this considering the customer-centric position of Dell and the nature of their business. However, his poignant statement is applicable to any business of any size. Having a vitally active and dynamic Customer Relations Policy should be crucial to your business.

If your staff are inadequately trained, this lack of insight into CRM only aggravates the problem. When we act as clients ourselves, we can clearly see this process in action.

There are companies that outsource their call center offshore to a country where employees have a peculiar accent and pronunciation not well understood by the average North American or European — and who simply follow a script they can't deviate from.

Common intelligence tells us that it shouldn't be this way. How a customer is dealt with reflects on the integrity of the brand, and the image of the company in the mind of the consumer.

Out of 362 leading companies surveyed, 80% believe they deliver a superior customer experience, but only 8% of their customers agree, states Bain & Company, a leading management consultancy firm. Moreover, the larger the market share of the firm in question, the greater the risk that this firm will take its customer base for granted.

REMARKABLE COMPANIES DELIVER REMARKABLE CRM

Dedicated firms deliver outstanding customer service, and this policy distinguishes the best companies from the pack. Consumer products can suffer from becoming mere commodities, with price used as the sole competitive advantage. Today, it is quick and easy to check the prices of competitors with your cell phone and price comparison apps.

As more people buy online, it is important to remember that your competitor is only one mouse click away. One way to overcome the price only differentiator, which eats away at the profits and does not generate brand loyalty, is for a company to consider building a lifelong relationship with each customer. To do so, requires that customers enjoy a positive and hassle-free transaction with each touch point. Take L.L. Bean, the outdoors outfitter and equipment supplier based in Freeport, Maine. If you buy any product and desire to return it for whatever reason, the firm will either refund or exchange the item. No questions asked and always with a smile. Now that's CRM.

The corporate goal should be to reduce or eliminate customer problems altogether. This tactic should begin prior to and during the first contact with the customer. All problems should be documented, reviewed and corrected without delay. Hiring the right people is vital, so is proper staff training, empowering staff to deliver a remarkable customer experience.

Top-performing companies also create processes that seek direct, immediate customer feedback. EBay employees known as "pinks" monitor the company's message boards, quickly learning which issues, complaints, and concerns may need attention. American Express calls customers who don't quickly activate their new cards to find out if they're having problems.

CUSTOMER ENGAGEMENT BUILDS EMOTIONAL BONDS

Engagement means creating involvement. Customer engagement is the effort taken by the company to involve their customers and the brand beyond regular purchase and use. Traditional marketing practices rarely encourage active participation of customers. Marketers are often quite content with the regular purchase of the product by the customers and the level of engagement with those customers is limited to handling inquiries, complaints and if any, loyalty programs.

Customer satisfaction is just the start. A business should aspire to engage its customers. Engaged customers ensure a sustained and profitable growth. Customer engagement is when a significant number of satisfied clients are proactively promoting the company to others with similar desires. It is not enough that they declare that they are willing to promote your business. Only when they go out to spread the word and encourage others to try your product or service do they prove that they have become engaged.

By listening to its customers, a business can learn a great deal. However, many struggle to convert these conversations into something that can really impact marketing, branding, and advertising in a meaningful way.

One valuable tactic is "Customer Collaboration" – private online communities made up of selected customers passionate about a company's products or services. Consider this strategy a customer advisory board by those who understand the brand and whose input can help the company make the most effective marketing decisions.

Gallup studies reveal that customers who are fully engaged represent an average 23% premium in terms of share of wallet, profitability, revenue, and relationship growth than the average customer. Actively disengaged customers represent a 13% discount in those same measures.

Simply put, engaged customers help you build your business.

There is much misunderstanding about the use of networking and social media such as LinkedIn, Viadeo, Facebook and Twitter. SM is not about marketing; it's about building meaningful relationships with your customers.

It acts as a complement to your marketing activities, and should be integrated according as a strategic position. Facebook has more than 800 million active users. Twitter has more than 100 million. Both networks have become the world's largest commercial channels and should be harnessed in order to influence prospects and to reinforce brand loyalty for existing customers.

If you do not use these networks or are unsure how to maximize their potential for your business, my advice is to learn. It is easy, but it takes time, patience, and a targeted strategic approach.

It's not enough for a company to simply add Facebook and Twitter buttons, expecting users will flock to "click". An excellent case-in-point for how older, established companies can put social media to work is, Samsung Electronics from South Korea.

It works for Samsung because the company is using social media through the methods that we, as consumers, want it to be used. The Samsung Tweets account on Twitter is not simply utilized for public relations pitches — it's a real tool being used for dialogue.

Samsung employees read reviews with comments left in a timely manner. As a result, the company appears to be learning from constant customer feedback. This in turn has deepened Samsung's consumer relationships. Social media is not a separate and distinct entity. Various departments work together online and offline to develop and implement plans devised to fully engage the community. In a nutshell, there are three activities to bring to mind:

Follow — Share — Engage.

EXCEEDING CUSTOMER EXPECTATIONS

Listening to the client and personalizing each relationship is crucial. Need a good example? Go to any Ralph Lauren store and you will see this strategy put into play to perfection.

Post sales should include building loyalty, continuous customer engagement and staying in touch with the patrons via newsletters, birthday cards, and special invitations to "Previews," or, Promotional or Themed events.

Milton Pedraza, CEO of the Luxury Institute in New York claims that "Luxury brands need to start focusing on what customer service means. They need to start to out-behave — not just outperform — the competition."

He further adds, "The customer experience at the store and website has to be extraordinary, and consistently so, in order for luxury consumers to develop long-term relationships."

It is clear that any innovative luxury brand building relationship strategy needs to engage their most committed customers by matching exclusivity and lifestyle. When this is achieved the brand has achieved engagement.

MEASURING THE CUSTOMER EXPERIENCE

Customer metrics allow companies to make certain their delivery continues to meet the needs of the target segments. Customer Engagement may be used to pursue customer loyalty as fully engaged customers feel an emotional bond with the brand and its employees. Compared to customer satisfaction, customer engagement offers a better measurement tool for increasing retention and other business results such as profits and return-on-investment.

"PeopleMetrics' Most Engaged Customer Study" whose results indicate that businesses with higher engagement levels do enjoy higher profits, a return-on-investment and market share has actually showed this. Companies, that are pursuing the love of their customers are more likely to be recommended, visited and returned to for additional purchases in the future.

EMPOWER YOUR EMPLOYEES & CUSTOMERS

World leading organizations create potential for growth by relentlessly improving their customer relationships. Such organizations have outperformed their competitors by 26% in gross margin and 85% in sales growth. Their customers spend more, return more often and stay longer.

Customer relationships are the result of all interactions, operational as well as marketing. Consumers will definitely share experiences with friends and family, so having a reputation for horrible customer service could kill the chance to build a relationship with consumers who have heard bad things through word-of-mouth. Engaging with customers is a two-way conversation. Connecting online and offline utilizing an analytic structure and acknowledging the value of each customer is the way moving forward.

Social networking sites are an ideal venue for brands to monitor what is being said about them. Those sites offer places for consumers to comment, praise, and criticize, as well as a way for them to follow brand promotions, events and a way to forward information to friends. While marketers seem to think about brands mainly in terms of whom their competitors are consumers tend to prefer brands that do something that plays a role in their lives.

Finding the right metric is an important step in a company's journey toward increasing customer engagement. However, measurement without action is pointless.

"People don't want to communicate with an organization or a computer. They want to talk to a real, live, responsive, responsible person who will listen and help them get satisfaction."

—Theo Michelson

A Philosophy Named CUSTOMER SERVICE — How to Refine it and Maintain It

Much is touted by companies about CUSTOMER SERVICE but surprisingly only a few actually deliver on their promises. At the outset, it appears that many lack a vital customer relations policy. Inadequate staff training amongst other factors further aggravates the problem. Picking up the telephone and calling certain companies, for example, can sometimes lead to an exasperating experience. People love to hate the phone tree experience where you have to go through a maze of menus until you eventually get to speak to a human — assuming you're lucky. It shouldn't have to be that way. How a customer is dealt with is a reflection of the brand — the image of the company in the consumers' mind.

"Customer service is a philosophy that starts with how a company or individual demonstrates their behavior in service and product," says Marvin Sadovsky, founder of Leadership Strategy LLC and author of Selling the Way Your Customer Buys.

The organization may call its division "customer relations", "customer experience", or other fancy designation. No matter what's decided to label it, its focus will be primarily on serving the customer. Yet, it won't make a difference if its executives/owners all the way down to those directly involved with clients, are not on the same wavelength. They all ought to be committed. This applies for business-to-consumer, as well as business-to-business markets, product or service industries.

REDEFINING AUTHENTIC CUSTOMER SERVICE/CARE

Customer service is nowadays offered in various venues — online, over the phone and in person. All these touch points should be superbly evaluated and finely tuned to deliver more than what a client expects. Dealing with a company's customer service center, for example, should be an efficient and pleasant experience. Same goes with online interaction and responding to e-mail inquiries in a timely manner along with elaborate answers. Online shoe retailer giant Zappos, which was recently acquired by Amazon, expects new hires to fit into their company culture. Great customer service doesn't start with the customer but rather from the character of the business ownership and its employees. It's that genuine quality that leads to lasting connections. So the first part of creating a service culture is to hire the people who have a desire to be service driven. Once the right candidates have been vetted, they should undergo a rigorous service orientation and retrained frequently so as to maintain their customer relations skills and prevent complacency. This is how a company creates an appropriate service oriented culture — it drives the message that it's a priority. CEO Tony Hsieh says Zappos hires in favor of personality over job experience every time. "One of our core values is to be humble. So if there is someone who is really talented, and we know they will make an immediate impact on our top or bottom line, but they are really egotistical, then we won't hire them," Hsieh says. In person, the front-line staffers at brick and mortar shops or offices should be well groomed, well spoken, patient and properly trained to delicately handle clients.

Ritz-Carlton employees spend 15 minutes every day talking about how they can make all guests feel like VIPs. They and the ones at Four Seasons are given a $2,000 budget per guest per day to do whatever needs to be done to satisfy guests and handle their glitches, if any. The return on investment for this allowance is much greater when you consider what a satisfied guest will spend over the years.

Companies in the consumer product market should make themselves easily accessible for any product inquiries by placing toll-free numbers visibly and in large font type on their packaging. Calls should be answered on the first or second ring and no phone tree. The trained person who handles the calls should be congenial, apologetic and non-argumentative. Amex and Apple, amongst others, are two such companies which seem to have achieved this.

CONSTANTLY RAISE THE STANDARD BAR — REMAIN THE BENCHMARK FOR YOUR SECTOR

Four Seasons Hotels runs the most popular luxury hotels in North America. So says the latest annual survey by J.D. Power and Associates, which questioned some 66,000 guests who stayed in a hotel between May 2008 and June 2009. Four Seasons scored 5/5 in all seven categories in which the hotels were assessed (reservations; check-in/checkout; guest room; food and beverage; hotel services; hotel facilities; and costs and fees).

According to the survey, not surprisingly, hotel guests increasingly want to be served the amenities they enjoy at home and at a fair price. They don't want to incur fees for extras such as parking or internet access. The survey revealed that there are customers who have a hard time understanding why a relatively inexpensive hotel offers free WiFi and bottled water while an expensive one charges excessively for these.

Another survey conducted by J.D. Power and Associates, for the automobile manufacturer customer satisfaction index study, placed Lexus in first place for its 2009 rankings. "The highest-performing brands differentiate themselves particularly in the service quality and service facility measures," said Jon Osborn, Research Director at J.D. Power and Associates.

"There are several practices where the highest-ranked brands consistently perform to help elevate customer service satisfaction levels, including providing prompt service appointments; greeting the customer immediately on arrival; knowing the vehicle's service history; returning vehicles to customers in a clean condition; and offering alternative transportation to customers leaving their cars for service. These courtesies may seem intuitive, but many dealers do not provide them consistently. We find that they are very effective in raising customer satisfaction, provided that the service work performed on the vehicle is also satisfactory."

CUSTOMER SATISFACTION CREATES LOYALTY

A principal way to survive in a downturn, like we're presently experiencing, is to maintain current customers. This repeat customer spends more, is more loyal over time, refers more — especially when rewarded in doing so, tends to be forgiving when a mistake is corrected swiftly, offers frequent word-of- mouth recommendations and is not price but value sensitive. This person is also cheaper to keep vs. finding a new one, and is increasingly more profitable over time.

Ironically, the best time to do great customer service is when a customer is upset. We are not supposed to let that happen in the first place: however, when it does occur, it's our chance to earn back the customer through our proper actions — damage control. Unfortunately, too many front-line employees fail to take advantage of this opportunity to regain the client's confidence in the brand/company.

Devise innovative ways to keep a following with your clients to maintain the enthusiasm for your brand, just as Apple has successfully achieved — most notably with the iPhone and iPod. The company makes certain that its after-sales service makes it easy for their customers to get help and advice from very knowledgeable and friendly staff. They have managed to make the use of their products and service the least annoying compared to their competitors.

CREATING THE ULTIMATE CUSTOMER EXPERIENCE

How you deliver can be as important as what you deliver. A high-end resort developer and operator, Kerzner International, has as its core value no. 1 as: "Blow away the customer." The company walks the talk by impressing its guests through grandiose entrances, facilities, overall ambiance and luxury amenities — then making absolutely certain that they are pampered throughout their stay. It's all an integrated, well-orchestrated and flattering process. Nothing is left to chance although it does take a coordinated team effort to make it all happen flawlessly.

INVOLVE CUSTOMERS — OBTAIN FEEDBACK FROM YOUR EMPLOYEES

Listen to your clients and personalize each relationship. Every individual is different and if you have one hundred clients, you may need one hundred different manners of approach with them. Listening and anticipating are the keys to success. Listen, observe what the client is looking for and sense their needs and taste. You need to demonstrate your genuine interest in them. Ask questions in order to understand their objective. Learn for which occasion they need a particular product. Understand their lifestyles and their families and grasp their physical or moral complexes and problems. We call this "aspiration" marketing.

As your company's most greatest asset, your employees are equally important in feeding you with information and new ideas. Encourage and inspire them to do so. After all, it's they who deal with clients daily and are most in touch with their needs.

TRAIN AND RE-TRAIN THE BRAND AMBASSADORS

Every person who does marketing, sales, product design or any other job that influences customers directly should spend at least a week or an hour a week answering the customer service lines, using the same tools your customer service people use. This shall provide them with firsthand experience, understanding and appreciation of their actual client requirements.

The importance of continuous training and injection of motivation coupled with incentives can't be overly emphasized. Provide your employees with the tools they need to perform their functions properly, implement a performance based bonus program, employee performance reviews, growth opportunities, as well as recognition awards.

HOW DO YOU MEASURE RESULTS?

Nowadays, it's recommended that you frequently verify and gauge your customer's experience by hiring mystery shoppers to make occasional phone inquiries and/or have them visit your business locations and rate you based on criteria you deem important. McDonald's and Berlitz have been doing this for the longest time. Your employees can easily be caught off-guard, but that shouldn't make them behave any differently than knowingly being observed by their superior.

Consider conducting customer surveys. Mercedes-Benz, for example, sends-out questionnaires to its clients on occasion seeking their opinion about their experiences with the sales consultant, service adviser, the dealership and the automobile itself. Their sincere efforts to go out of their way for their customers, through various actions, clearly demonstrate that they are obsessed with upholding their prestige brand reputation.

Great customer service is when organizations are going the extra mile with their employees giving more than they have to. This should also apply to the public service sector. Conversely, that's a whole other topic which makes for a subsequent yet intriguing section.

"Design is the method of putting form and content together. Design, just as art, has multiple definitions; there is no single definition. Design can be art. Design can be aesthetics. Design is so simple, that's why it is so complicated."

— Paul Rand

"Companies need to create emotional innovation in order to create moods that attract and addict customers"

— Kjell Nordstrom

Chapter VI: Design and Innovation

The Essence of Creative Consumer Product and Packaging Design

When you head to the grocery store to pick up a product such as cereal, do you purchase the same one each and every time or, like many consumers, are you comparing and contemplating about which one to grab?

When presented with a large range of choices to fulfill a need, it is in human nature to become confused, thus the inability to quickly make a choice. When we spend too much time comparing the plethora of options we are presented with, the functional differences between each of them soon become blurry. Once the functional differences lose importance, the peripheral aspects take precedence. This means that whichever product's ad, spokesperson, or packaging color stands out favorably in our minds will most likely influence our product purchase.

What does this signify for those responsible for branding and communications for such low-involvement products?

Axe, a brand of male grooming products owned by the British/Dutch company Unilever is a good example of how this can be addressed.

Their marketing messages are well-known and hold a great amount of recall. They are likely to be quite popular in the deodorant and body spray isle where men are faced with more brands than they can count, and where functional superiority or inferiority takes a back seat.

Those factors differ for high-involvement goods, such as in cars, watches and so on, where the customer is not likely to make a grab-and-go purchase. In these cases, functionality, brand values and associations begin to play a key role.

CONNECTING INDUSTRY WITH CONSUMERS

Product designers' work on new products with two aspects in mind: functionality and aesthetics. Through their work, designers connect the industry with consumers by translating a concept into something that adds extra value to consumers.

A competent design team should have an excellent understanding of people, culture, and societies. This knowledge is applied to its deep knowledge about design and includes, but is not limited to:

- Materials;
- Components;
- Production Techniques;
- Practical Experience;
- Financial Insight.

In this way, products are developed that not only have an appealing design and bring out emotion, but are also practical and of high quality. The products will have the right combination of feel, detailing and ease of usage. Pricing will then determine the value equation.

CREATIVE PACKAGING BOOSTS SALES

Packaging is as important as product itself. The main objective of packaging design is attracting a buyer's attention to the product. Along with making the product look amazing, it should prompt and influence the customer into buying the actual product as looks do matter.

No matter how good the product is, if the packaging is dull and inferior-looking it may compromise the sales of its contents. Consequently, modern, creative and clever packaging design plays a major role in inspiring and selling any product. Packaging design should include labeling which expresses and communicates key information to the end-user such as benefits, product information, usage directions and perhaps a story.

Some consumer product companies are using a more educated market approach. For instance, to stand-out on the crowded supermarket shelves they introduce art in the printing of their packages and/or labels inviting the consumer to reach-out for the product to learn more about it.

A case in point, after more than two decades in the limelight, California's Kenwood Vineyards' highly acclaimed Artist Series Cabernet Sauvignon reigns as a premier marriage of fine art and fine wine. The combination of the fine art of wine making with the work of contemporary artists creates an elegant, easily identifiable package, while promoting beautiful artwork at the same time.

STYLISH AND ECO-FRIENDLY

Many modern companies these days make every effort to produce both "green" products and packaging that meet with modern environmental standards so as to reduce their carbon footprint — which includes the reduction of the size of its packaging. This demonstrates eco-friendliness which can bolster their image and attract additional new clients — especially those who are environmentally sensitive.

DESIGN INSTIGATES SUSTAINABLE COMPETITIVE ADVANTAGE

The approach to creativity is the way an artist might stand before a new canvas, on which a beautiful painting can be crafted. Staff who work in a creative environment should be given plenty of leeway to utilize their full potential — the freedom to flourish. Not doing so limits their artistic talent and deprives the company from taking a leap at the competition.

By having a good understanding about materials, production techniques and manufacturers, striking designs can be created that assure loyal partnerships between consumers and manufacturers. This saves marketing costs in the short term and creates more stability in the long term.

The primary goal of packaging design is to entice customers' attention. For this purpose, package designs cannot simply inform the customers, but also provoke feelings and communicate emotions. An effective packaging looks attractive, impresses with its creativity and is not simply appealing to have on the shelf. As a result, it stands out in an increasingly competitive marketplace.

Amongst other impressive statistics, stocks of design-led firms outperformed the FTSE 100 by 200%! That should be compelling evidence enough to make product designs consumer appealing.

If a manufacturer is to create and produce new products, as well as re-design existing ones, why not bulk up with creativity as proved by the French industrial designer Philippe Starck? His "Juicy Lucy" manufactured by Alessi is a perfect example of how you can take a "mundane" orange juice squeezer and turn it into an iconic design "must have."

To get the "wow" factor of emotional branding, play back Apple's advert campaigns to yourself for inspiration, and witness the genius of style, design, and function harmonized to capture the imagination of an entire planet.

"Luxury CEOs need to know how the target market perceives their brand's reputation and that of their competitors' (LBSI), and how customers rate their brand experience and competitors' experiences (LCEI)."

— Milton Pedraza

"Illusion is in the air as luxury goods companies, like magicians, try to preserve both their differentiation and sales, favoring the dream rather than the reality of rarity. This dream is a multidimensional concept built on clever management of the information delivered to customers. But the dream is here to stay — if only because luxury firms have always been experts in the art of selling illusion."

— *Business Strategy Review,* Autumn 2003 - Volume 14, Issue 3 - The great pretenders: the magic of luxury goods

Chapter VII: The Luxury Domain

Defining the Luxury Brand

Open any quality fashion or lifestyle magazine, and you will see how brands conceptualize and package luxury. The hype is deafening, and in reality can be quite confusing. Everyone wants "luxury" brands, and from a marketing point of view they defy sales trends and seem recession proof.

As consumers, we want to be made to feel special. Definitions of "luxury" can vary enormously and depend on who you ask and in what context. The term "Luxury" has never been easy to define. In my view, it's a mysterious and elusive concept. Studies highlight that no one is immune and when properly executed makes products and services highly desirable by broad market segments.

To put things into perspective, I will discuss the nature of luxury, and how luxury and premium brands differ in the marketplace although both types of products and services can be targeted to similar audiences.

WHY LUXURY BRANDS?

The first key point to understand is that people buy luxury brands for a multitude of reasons. In general these brands are expensive and are targeted to high net worth individuals and people who have high levels of DPI. The desirability to possess is based on the consumers need for high quality, exclusivity, craftsmanship, precision and innovation. They involve issues of self-perception and self-worth. These underlying reasons lie at the subconscious level of the individual and include points such as peer recognition and approval, status, and the envy one's inner circle.

In the services sector such as in tourism and business travel think 5-star hotels and resorts. We all appreciate the ambiance and "feel good" experience. In medicine, plastic surgery can offer illusions of "eternal youth" and enhanced aesthetics.

Luxury products can be broken down into three categories:

Prestige brands such as Louis Vuitton, Rolex, Mercedes-Benz and Cartier represent the highest form of craftsmanship and command a loyal consumer following that is not affected by trends. Due to their pedigree, they are well-established as status symbols. For example, If Daniel Craig or George Clooney wear an Omega watch in an advert or film, sales immediately spike.

Premium brands are those like Polo Ralph Lauren, Calvin Klein and Tommy Hilfiger, which aspire to be luxury and prestige brands but their marketing is geared more to, as terms, an affluent mass market or as mass-luxury brands.

Fashion brands on the other hand are those that address the masses and whose designs can be seasonal. Call them the "hot trends" or "fads" of the immediate moment.

It's foolish for a company to think that by simply launching a product with a "luxury" label attached will make their targeted market flock to it. It takes diligent planning, execution, clever strategic marketing and PR buzz alongside ambiance and finesse. To be perceived as unique, luxury products and services should have an aura of mystery surrounding them. Interestingly enough, the more ubiquitous the product and the more accessible, the less the "mystery" concept holds true.

THE DAZZLE FACTOR

A brand that is committed to be a player in the luxury domain should endeavor to build long-lasting loyalty by creating products that resonate with customers on an emotional level. It's what we call the "Dazzle" factor.

Glamour is another important ingredient. It is the impression of attraction or fascination that a particularly luxurious or elegant appearance creates — an impression which is better than reality.

The ambiance you create is one of your best marketing tools. The aesthetic appeal to human senses, the feel of your business and the brand you create is your image. Along with great service, it is one of the most important reasons customers will choose to do business with you on frequent basis. Invite customers to truly feel the brand experience by adding character. This is accomplished by connecting the emotions to a product or service, and infusing it with a tangible and intangible essence that remain in the customers' minds.

It's natural to expect luxury brand purchasers accustomed to being pampered. VIPs as they're known to be labeled, they're also used to having access to the hottest entertainment events, parties and sports venues. A brand known to deliver on those types of unique experiences is *Quintessentially*, a world leading private members' club, which has a global concierge network that provides such a service 24 hours a day, 365 days a year including specialist advice, insider access and benefits to absolutely anything you can think of, from property, art, bespoke fashion and fine wine, through to luxury travel, security, event production and publishing.

LUXURY VS. PREMIUM

Luxury is self-expression, an exceptional experience and a feeling of sense of emotion. There is also a difference between a "luxury" and a "premium" product but they can be both — as in a tailored-made fine wool suit for example by Camps de Luca in Paris.

Luxury product pricing is related to scarcity, brand and storytelling. Premium goods, on the other hand, are expensive variants of commodity goods — pay more, get more. It's the craftsmanship and quality along with the pedigree of the product. Plenty of brands get in trouble because they can't figure-out which one they represent.

THE IMPACT OF NICHE AND LIFESTYLE

What distinguishes luxury automobiles from others are the so-called "bells and whistles," comfort, additional safety features, leather heated seats, ergonomics, styling and performance to name a few. Besides the car itself, the overall awe-inspiring experience is crucial. From the moment one purchases the vehicle and during servicing.

One of the most respected brands in the world is BMW. This ever-growing brand has been successful in creating a cult, a body of owners that are extremely faithful, devoted and *committed to their brand*. BMW stands for *fine engineering and* "The Ultimate Driving Machine". Those principles have maintained consistency over time and across its entire range, which guarantees its authenticity, its attraction, its mystique, as well as its spark.

With women's designer handbags, it's the craftsmanship including a confidence booster to its owner as the bag screams to the world, you are unique. The Sophia Coppola collection at Louis Vuitton and the "Birkin" bag at Hermes are notable examples with the latter design house producing limited quantities to generate and guarantee exclusivity through scarcity, i.e. limited editions.

As for high-end condominiums, it's the sought after location, the trendy architecture/design, its facilities and overall experience. It's the impression that it's irreplaceable. Selling only "the" amenities is kind of outdated.

People want more than that. Instead they are looking for self-definition and a sense of belonging when choosing to live in a certain property. The "Trump" name is renowned for its cachet with its properties as they redefine luxury. From the elegant design of the residential units and spectacular lobbies, to the distinguished quality of services and amenities that are available around the clock for its residents, the organization has a reputation for detail.

DIFFERENTIATING "NOUVEAU-RICHE" FROM "OLD MONEY"

"Old Money", with persons from families who have been wealthy for multiple generations, has its established habits and favored brands. It's deep-rooted and less concerned with peer pressure or keeping-up with the Jones's.

Unfortunately, research is showing that "old money" is not only becoming scarce but also buying less. For this reason, to survive and grow, luxury brands should be focusing their marketing efforts on the "Nouveau-Riche". This term is used to identify people who have acquired considerable wealth within their generation. The newly rich spend money to assert their freedom and self-expression and while doing so, enjoy flaunting their success, whereas "Old Money" behaves more conservatively.

IT'S MUCH MORE THAN SIMPLY "PACKAGING AND PRESENTATION"

It's not enough to simply introduce and sell a luxury brand surrounded by a fancy store with design-inspired display cases. The attitude, product knowledge and overall delivery/ presentation of the product by the sales consultant/brand ambassador all play an equally important role.

A study by The Luxury Institute finds that Burberry and Bottega Veneta excel far better than other companies at having enthusiastic brand ambassadors in their stores who are interested in helping customers. This was one of the key findings of the report titled, "Leading edge insights into the world of the wealthy."

Mystery shoppers commissioned by The Luxury Institute said that the layout, location and atmospheres of the Burberry and Bottega Veneta stores were what clients appreciated most.

"A customer-centric culture is something that is a self-reinforcing system that creates consistently extraordinary customer experience," said Milton Pedraza, CEO of The Luxury Institute, New York.

"Service values, service standards and education on operational and cultural functions need to be in place." He further added, "Luxury brands should have a set of service values. They need to educate and hire the right people. Whenever a new store opens, brands need to make sure they test employees for personality. They need to be educated in the customer experience and the culture of the brand, not just how to work a register," Furthermore, he stated, "We know every luxury brands CEO gets luxury brand customer service".

EXCLUSIVITY IS KEY TO BRANDING

Classic brands such as Coca Cola and Pepsi Cola put emphasis on their differentiation with their competitors. They specify its positioning then convey it through its products, its services, its price, its distribution and finally through its communication.

With genuine luxury brands, it's not the same approach. Being unique is what counts, not any comparison with a competitor. JN Kapferer and V. Bastien, authors of the book, "*The Luxury Strategy: Break the Rules of Marketing to Build Luxury Brands*", succinctly state that,

"Luxury is the expression of a taste, of a creative identity, of the intrinsic passion of a creator; luxury makes the bald statement 'this is what I am,' not 'that depends' — which is what positioning implies.

What made the Christian Lacroix brand is its image of bright sunshine, full of this designer's bright, vivid colors', suffused with the culture of the Mediterranean; it certainly is not concerned with its positioning with respect to this or that established designer."

The role of advertising a luxury product or service is not to sell at all. Unlike traditional ads where the text makes the sales pitch, with luxury adverts, it's about refinement. A large photo of the product in a lifestyle setting is displayed along with a brief story line with some mystery.

When you visit a Porsche dealer, the sales consultant will talk to you about racetracks, describe road-holding capabilities, build-up a fascinating story — after which time he/she will tell you about reliability, and the "technical" details.

To be successful in luxury marketing today, marketers should target and combine experiential marketing to attract and retain customers with emphasis on the individual lifestyle.

The Polo Ralph Lauren corporation, which was named "Luxury Marketer of the Year" for 2010, knows a thing or two about successful luxury marketing. The runner-up was Louis Vuitton, and third-place was awarded to Burberry.

The accolade was won on the strength of an integrated strategy which included interactive marketing while continuing its rich and distinct brand story in print and beyond — all leading to double-digit growth in 2010.

"Creating a luxury brand is one thing, but maintaining its marketing aura across good times and bad, traditional media and new, takes genius and Ralph Lauren," said Mickey Alam Khan, Editor in Chief of *Luxury Daily*, New York. "Ralph Lauren's marketing has become a byword for excellence with consistent creative messaging and an effective call to action in an era where luxury brands struggle to retain their mystique," he added.

EXPERIENCE IS FUNDAMENTAL

Luxury isn't about price anymore. It's about spending on brands that are authentic and meaningful through function, design, and intrinsic value received.

Luxury products must provide the right experience. Sophisticated customers want products that impress their senses, touch their hearts and stimulate their minds — which they can relate to and can incorporate into their lifestyles. The degree to which a company is able to deliver a desirable customer experience is vital.

While public relations and advertising in selected media has been the mainstay, astute marketers have also adopted prestige event sponsorship which offers exposure to the right targeted audience. Mercedes-Benz with its New York Fashion Week is one such example.

Craftsmanship is making a comeback too, as people look for better, longer-lasting things. In the past years it was about "collecting" quantities of things, but now, it's about exclusivity and quality things, that please. Design must be timeless for longer visual enjoyment.

At this crossroads, "luxury" and "premium" meet at the junction in unity of purpose.

"Whether it's the visionary architecture, the stunning location, the meticulous details in a hand-carved banister, we take great pleasure in discovering and bringing to life all the things that make a home unique, and in artfully uniting these special places with those who will cherish them as we do.

Memories, relationships, treasured possessions — homes are repositories of the things that matter most. To market a distinctive home requires uncommon knowledge and resources."

— Lew Geffen | Sotheby's International Realty

Luxury Condominium Project Marketing: Challenging Conventional Wisdom is Heads-Up Branding

Luxury real estate projects should be marketed in similar fashion to what Cartier, BMW or Rolex are achieving. This marketing approach should be based on demographic and psycho-graphic analysis which equates to extreme attention to customer experience and service; integrated marketing across every touch point, as well as to every function and channel. The formula is straightforward: the right brand, the right location, the right product and the right ambiance for the right customer.

THE PROJECT LOCATION AS A SHOWROOM

Create a display area on the property that allows your potential buyers to have the emotional experience of what living in the building would be like. It's about evoking and engaging the consumer. Creating a sense of a desirable lifestyle. Have the showroom accessible for extended hours each day, seven days a week for those whose schedule is volatile.

Seduce and dazzle your clients with the emotional "wow" factor. Create an experience. Very good examples of this are what the "One&Only" resorts and New York City luxury real estate marketing project guru, Michael Shvo, have managed to do respectively. This helps in spreading the word. Associate the property with renowned names/brands/designers as part of the cachet. That's what helps trigger a sale and at prices beyond what one would expect to pay for the property.

"IRREPLACEABLE PROPERTY MARKETING" — UNIQUE & HARD TO EMULATE

Make the look and experience authentic with the impression that it's irreplaceable. People want to feel they own something that has a personality and a story. That means more than just the usual appliance upgrades or adding a health club.

New developments and modernized properties should be design conscious and unique — able to cater to the discerning crowd. They should be promoted and presented with panache, flair, color, style and hype than anyone else. A professional marketer, with refined brand image skills and savoir-faire in the luxury real estate domain, can develop and execute a strategy that will make the project and its identity speak and sing for itself.

Moreover, the practitioner should be able to reduce the risk for the developer through a pre-sale process by employing a launch strategy that builds and consolidates demand in advance of a selection event. This methodology allows for decisions to be made about pricing and creates controls. If all conditions are correct, this can lead to higher return on investment (R.O.I.) and a shorter sales cycle.

Attract, Impress and Close

As with any marketing and sales objective, the former aides the latter as they work collectively. Soon as the potential buyer has been compelled to arrive at the "showroom' he/she should be impressed and persuaded by the ambiance, the "presenters/consultants" and the story-telling to the extent that the sale ought to close with little effort. It's a team effort, though every player on the team should be trained, competent and on the same page.

Property marketing is essentially "Show Business" with the aim at "Theatre" along with all the levels of drama and passion the brand should be fully capable of carrying.

"The quality of life is determined by its activities."
— **Aristotle**

Upscale Restaurant Marketing with an Attitude — Seducing & Retaining Discerning Patrons through Lean and Challenging Times

What do we conjure-up in our minds when we see or hear the expressions, "upscale restaurant" and "high-end restaurant"? Undoubtedly, they denote "fine dining." Expand those adjectives further and we think of pricey, presentation, ambiance and service — including restaurants which could be described as "trendy" and "nouveau" anything. An upscale restaurant should strive for top ratings in every category which enhances its image and reputation. Therefore, focus is multi-dimensional as in good food, extensive wine selection, atmosphere, including striking and tidy washrooms, choice furniture, tableware, cutlery, and glassware along with courteous and seasoned staff. It's easy to see that these essentials combined can amount to sort of a "show" business within the dining experience.

Despite the recession still lingering and value with premium replacing luxury, fine dining is in the process of redefining itself swiftly. Tourists, special events/celebrations and corporate dining have all scaled back their generous spending. The truth of the matter is that the desire for great food and service will never change — no matter how bad the economy gets. There will always be folks who have the desire to indulge the highest level of culinary experience. It simply becomes a much smaller market where additional creativity becomes essential to capture those discerning clients. Menu offerings for business lunches are also being injected with "a la carte" prices which present tremendous value for money going as low as $20 — provided the diners take advantage during lunch hours only.

ADJUSTING TO THE NEW REALITY

Shrewd owners have come to realize that they must adapt to the new economic realities. For this reason, they have revamped their prices, menus, as well as innovated and focused on lean operations. Some are also tweaking their marketing strategy to generate enhanced results with less to spend.

Drew Nieporent, co-founder of New York's Myriad Restaurant Group, owner/operator of such up-scale establishments as Corton, Nobu, Tribeca Grill, Mai House and Centrico, agrees that fine dining isn't going anywhere.

"All of us in the foodservice business feel there is some sort of place for fine dining, but we also pioneered the *casualization* of it." "That doesn't mean we want it to go extinct, but we have relaxed the rules to where dress codes or a pretentious experience have disappeared."

RE-TOOLING THE MARKETING MACHINE TO CONVEY THE DINING EXPERIENCE — PERCEPTION IS EVERYTHING

The central theme for a "lifestyle" fine dining establishment should be a distinctive style that you can spot a mile away. As a primary rule, a prospective or existing owner definitely needs a passion for epicurean food coupled by an instinctive understanding of what people want and willing to pay a premium for. In favor of a growing customer base of loyal patrons, this is the solid foundation that will support the building blocks of the food establishment.

One of the finest case studies of an astute marketer and operator in this domain is serial restaurant entrepreneur Peter Morentzos based in the predominantly French speaking city of Montreal — renowned for its impressive array of dining establishments. As a concept and menu originator, as well as owner and operator of renowned high-end dining establishments such as *Queue de Cheval* ("Horses Tail") and *La Brasserie Le Pois Penche*, amongst others, details are everything to Pete (as he's known to his friends). His interpretation of such sensory elements have inspired him to develop well over 13 unique restaurant concepts and build over 65 restaurants in 20 years. His talent is in the way he creates timeless concepts that tap into a distinct memory from one's past. One of the best examples of this is *La Brasserie Le Pois Penche* which opened in December 2007, but still manages to look like it has been there for 100 years. Personally responsible in all aspects from conception, interior design, food and wine development, staff selection and service, Peter has created a unique brand of trend-setting, thematic restaurant concepts. Elements of Morentzos' style found in each thriving venue include high ceilings, exhibition kitchens, trendy "menus-du-marché" and eclectic music — all used as strategic weapons to excite and seduce guests. Based on the insight that dining offers a "form of entertainment or art," each one carries with it a sense of event and celebration. In the end, it is his relentless curiosity, drive, and generosity of Morentzos, himself, which are truly key to the personality of his empire. This is in fact the secret to his success that many others are keen to emulate. However, execution of all the components is vital but not as effortless as they appear.

THE PURSUIT OF SUCCESS — SALES — MARKETING — BRANDING — PUBLIC RELATIONS — EVENT PLANNING

Marketing and sales are the corner-stone and driving force of all restaurant concepts, let alone upscale dining establishments. Differentiating restaurants in all marketplaces gives them a distinctly competitive edge. There is the need for a creative direction and graphics expertise to build a strong and lasting brand and an effective market penetration. Sales literature and marketing material should be conceived and executed either by in-house talented staff or outsourced to a select agency which understands the philosophy of the dining experience. The marketing division/staff should conceive, develop and execute all the establishment's events, charity or otherwise. The department should be responsible for choreographing a marketing blitz in the form of radio and print advertising and informational pamphlets to be circulated within hotels and established press contacts. It's important to stress that the marketing activities of the restaurant should be well versed in both B2B and B2C with the former having emphasis in the hotel and tourism sectors in general. You could do some promotions with strategic partners like florists, hotel getaways, jewelry stores, event planners or other vendors who cater to special occasions. Perhaps cater to the top businesses in your area by offering special deals to offer a world-class, deal-closing dining experience. Offer extras that can make the visit a special experience — it's got to be more than just the food.

IMPLEMENTING A CUSTOMER RETENTION POLICY

Once the creative marketing campaign has accomplished its mission to attract the customers to the establishment, the dining experience has to equal or surpass the expectations of the diners. Moreover, we should remind ourselves that customer retention should work as follows:

Service: Great service is offered to customers at every touchpoint (i.e. client booking process, welcome when guests arrive, politeness of waiters/waitresses, great food, its presentation and the manner in which it is served along with a post dining farewell). None should be left to chance as this could spell the difference between a one-time or repeat visit and affect word-of- mouth advertising.

Relationship: How do your staff communicate with patrons? Advertisements must be appealing and memorable. Client gripes should be handled promptly, cordially and discreetly from other patrons.

Public Relations: Your reputation in the area is also vital to retention. It's not often that a restaurant will undertake PR, but it's a practical, virtually low-cost, believable/earned and quite effective. Think charity events held at the restaurant, charitable donations, helping a local kids charity and even making bold moves with unusual themed events that will create buzz similar to what a premium steak house organizes almost once a year with its swanky "Mardi Bra" fund raising event.

The problem with many restaurants is the lack of contact with their customers. It's worth considering an investment in a CRM (client relationship management) software program or start with a simple spreadsheet with customer details and the dates of visits. This is a good way to track how often a client returns for another visit (weekly, monthly, quarterly etc.) and if for some reason they are late for their "usual" booking, a postcard can easily be sent to remind them the restaurant is still there to welcome them. A CRM tool can also be used as a database for sending Christmas cards, reminders about Valentines and so on.

Consumers have Spoken — Restaurants at the Podium

In a recent Gallup poll, Americans stated they are keenest on the computer industry, with the restaurant business and hard-working farmers not far behind. This is encouraging, yet not surprising as people enjoy their dining experiences — especially with upscale restaurants when it comes to indulging themselves. This type of news should give comfort to competent restaurant owners who are prepared to raise the bar with their innovative methods of attracting and retaining new and existing patrons — regardless of the state of the economy. Know your market, your competitors, adapt, pursue a wow effect, strategize and flawlessly execute. Avoid complacency.

*"Some people think luxury is the opposite of poverty.
It is not. It is the opposite of vulgarity."*

— Coco Chanel

Embracing a New Paradigm Shift in the Luxury Product Domain — Post Recession

Today's consumer spending pattern has shifted. As high-end consumers everywhere have suddenly curtailed their appetite for luxury goods, what was once considered a recession-proof industry has been hit hard. Early this year, in Tokyo, Louis Vuitton canceled plans for what would have been its largest and most glittery store anywhere while Chanel announced the layoff of 200 temporary employees — which the daily newspaper *Le Parisien* called a bombshell.

No category in the luxury domain has been spared a significant drop in sales including fine spirits, watches and yachts. Suddenly, the perception on the street is that luxury goods are considered a sign of immorality, superficiality and ostentation. Restraint and modesty are in.

On the indulgence services side, lifestyle spending rose on health and wellness but dropped on luxury travel.

WEALTH HAS DROPPED EVERYWHERE

The wealth of the world's richest people fell by almost a fifth in 2010 to $33 trillion, according to the *2009 World Wealth Report* from Merrill Lynch and Capgemini. Their wealth declined by more than 20% in North America, Europe and Asia, but by a bit less in Africa and the Middle East. Latin America's rich were the least affected: they lost 6% of their wealth, and the number there fell by less than 1%. In North America, which had a large proportion of people just above the $1 Million threshold, the ranks slimmed by 19%.

LUXURY VS. SUPERIOR QUALITY

Luxury goods are needlessly expensive — their price is not related to performance. Instead, the price is related to scarcity, brand and storytelling. Premium goods, on the other hand, are expensive and higher grade versions of commodity goods. You pay more to get more — most notably, quality.

"We are seeing the consumer move away from the prestige purchase, the blingy, the flash, to quality," says Mary Beth Whitfield, Senior Vice President of the consulting firm Retail Forward. "Consumers will still resonate with something that is marketed as premium or classic."

DILEMMAS BRING NEW OPPORTUNITIES

Plenty of brands are in trouble right now because they're not sure which one they represent. One suggestion is to find your heritage, your traditional values, as well as your commitment to craft and quality, or simply make up those attributes if you have to. Michael Silverstein of the Boston Consulting Group believes that luxury brands traditionally have competed on three dimensions — technology, function, and emotion— and says that the battle is now shifting more toward technology and function, away from "lifestyle and mystique." "The best companies," Silverstein explains, "are investing in technical and functional capability."

REDEFINING THE BRAND AND ITS ALLURE

Brands are moving beyond just logos and packaging. They should be equally perceived as practical. Core luxury consumers are evolving towards seeking for a more meaningful story and some luxury brands are beginning to hear this clearly. Instead of "self-indulgence" their clients prefer "sharing the pleasures of life" and replacing "conspicuous consumption" with "conscious consumption."

Prestige brands need to take immediate steps to develop plans to regain lost customers. Effective planning requires a detailed understanding of how consumer behavior and attitudes have changed. The feasible strategy should then be executed in a timely manner. Luxury purveyors need to recapture the sales volume that has been lost when the economic circumstances have forced consumers to reconsider their purchasing priorities. Luxuries items which are perceived as "nice-to-haves" (or non-essential) seem to be frowned-upon as consumers need to cut spending.

PUT AWAY THOSE PRICE CUTTING SCISSORS

What high-end brands should not do is get into a panic and start discounting prices simply for the sake of surviving the downturn, because consumers often look to price as a signal of quality. By cutting prices a brand may undermine perceptions of quality. Lowering price should be the tactic of last resort. By cutting prices, companies encourage customers to regard the depressed price as normal, making it very difficult to return prices to previous levels when the economy eventually recovers. As an alternative, offer a gift item (of lesser value) with the purchase or complimentary tickets to an attractive arts event or perhaps a gift certificate to a fine restaurant.

A prestige brand should be perceived as worth paying more while making certain it has an emotional connection. Luxury will survive, as long as there will always be those wealthy who are willing to pay to possess an exclusive product they can admire. Conspicuous consumption will always exist, though not in the same degree as we have witnessed prior to the recession.

For luxury brands to thrive, as they have been this past, they need to look beyond just the elite demographic. They need to start focusing and catering to the mass affluent who are a group much larger than the super-rich and who have been most affected by the recent economic upheaval. The mass affluent today are defined as clients with investible assets of US$100,000-$1 Million. This category is willing to trade-up for items that are emotionally important to it.

"During a political campaign everyone is concerned with what a candidate will do on this or that question if he is elected except the candidate; he's too busy wondering what he'll do if he isn't elected."

— Everett Dirksen

Business Outside of the Corporation

How to Run an Effective Political Campaign — a Synopsis for the Aspiring Candidate

A political campaign can be an exciting and challenging experience especially with the great deal of circumstances that will transpire between the start of the campaign until Election Day. Whether a person is running as an independent or, an active member or leader of a party, to be effective requires the same skill set as that of running a business. Disregard how the public service sector operates since it's bureaucratic and a process driven entity.

The difference between winning and losing is what goes on inside the campaign.

DECISION: WHY RUN IN THE FIRST PLACE?

No one runs for office alone. There is a heavy reliance on the people around the aspiring candidate. With that in mind, the first thing a prospective candidate usually does is to host a small gathering in his/her home to pitch the idea and see what kind of support might be available. If the support is sufficient and we presume that the candidate has a clean background and credibility intact, the ultimate decision then rests with that person as to whether or not he/she should make the commitment to run for office. One needs to carefully weigh the pros and cons since a campaign is very time-consuming and constantly drains one's energy. Compensation, if an incentive, should not be the main motivation. Privileges, networking and serving local constituents can be very beneficial, as well as satisfying. Part of or an additional reason to seek office can be dissatisfaction with the way the public sector is run and/or passion about certain issues.

Support from the candidate's family is imperative, as long hours and a volatile schedule will most certainly be expected. Equally important is to obtain assurances from a group of potential supporters who can add credibility to the campaign and spread the word to their spheres of influence.

Being organized, energetic, articulate, versatile, patient, persevering, tenacious, consistent, well-informed and persuasive are important characteristics the candidate should possess. The list may seem like a tall order; however, members of his/her competent team can compensate for any deficits/weak points.

RESEARCH: KNOWLEDGE IS AN ASSET — PARTICULARLY WHEN APPLIED

For starters, it is important to first know the issues involved in the office sought. By identifying the specific needs of the community or beyond the candidate wishes to serve, this person will put himself/herself in a position to do the maximum for his/her potential political constituency.

Depending on how involved the candidate is with issues of public policy, the research process can vary. Regardless, of the sources and methods one will use at his/her disposal to gather factual information, the person must have a very good command of all the important issues he/she will be facing and managing.

ORGANIZATION AND COORDINATION: KEY ELEMENTS AND STRUCTURE OF THE CAMPAIGN

Like every project and endeavor, the key to a successful campaign is good planning. This can be done before or after establishing a campaign team, although it is often helpful to have input from the campaign team during the planning stages. It helps to ensure that all members of the team are on the same page throughout the campaign. The more comprehensive the plan, the fewer decisions will have to be made in the heat of the moment and the team will have a greater capacity to adapt and respond throughout the campaign period.

One of the most significant factors in the success of any political campaign is the number, quality and commitment of volunteers used to guide, implement and promote the campaign. Volunteers have many roles to play, and getting the right person to fill each of these roles is essential to success. The number of volunteers needed in a campaign will depend on factors such as the size and scope of the campaign, the number of staff and the recommendations of the campaign advisors/consultants. Once all the volunteers are in place, the next task is to keep them interested and involved in the campaign. They need to believe in the mission of the organization. Without this belief and passion for what the organization is doing, it will be hard to keep volunteers motivated.

Another valuable campaign and planning tool is to create an information database. This should contain names, phone numbers and e-mails of potential supporters who say they will support the candidate or work for him/her during the campaign and to contact them for their unequivocal support. It is important to follow through with anyone who offers to contribute their time to the campaign. The campaigner can stay in touch with those in the campaign database via e-mail. On the day of the election, it will be useful to contact all of the identified supporters and ensure that they will be heading to the polling station.

A time-line is also one of the best planning tools. It is a chronological list of tasks, events, interviews, deadlines and other events of importance which details what must be done throughout the campaign period. This helps ensure that nothing is overlooked.

PLATFORM AND SELF-BRANDING/IMAGE: CREATING A DISTINCT IDENTITY

There are candidates seeking office due to strong feelings on a single or several issues. However, if the voters don't share the candidate's strong feeling, the candidate needs to determine if he/she is comfortable focusing on other issues. Likewise, decisions need to be made about comfort levels with negative messages including advertising. Will the campaign refer to their opponent(s) in any way? If so, what issues are fair play? When such questions are answered, can the campaign put together a realistic strategy?

A candidate should make promises he/she believes in, take a stand on issues, but does not promise that position will be implemented. Moreover, this person should promise to stand up for certain projects not the outcome, do as much research as possible into every issue and promise being made. Most importantly, emphasis should be a value-based platform rather than a specific promise regarding an issue.

Branding is the promise that the campaign is making. It is demonstrated by the campaign logo, slogan, website, brochures, and direct mail campaigns. Further, it is demonstrated by the way a candidate's staff answers the phones and the manner in which the candidate conducts himself/herself during public events. It is infused into all actions and interactions. For an effective marketing approach, a candidate should focus on being distinctive. Self-branding with strong yet meaningful taglines that people can relate to and a logo all ought to be considered. In addition, the tag line must boast a recall factor. Clear, succinct and consistent messaging must be printed on all of the campaign literature.

This can be accomplished by seeking professional help for graphics and signage.

Along with branding, the personal name, a candidate's differentiation can also be branded. This should include, communicating reasons why the campaigner is a better choice than the incumbent and other opponents, if any.

FUNDRAISING ACTIVITY: CREATING A REALISTIC CAMPAIGN BUDGET

Once a candidate knows the circumstances of the constituency he/she wishes to lead, that person will want to arrange for a funding scheme. Where funding for the average local campaign likely requires very little funding, campaigns for higher office such as big city mayor positions, money will be key to success. It's a good idea to consider local businessmen, investors and party committee members; people who are likely to hold the same views as the candidate often find it a good investment to back someone like-minded. Of course, it is important to note that rules and laws apply to campaign fund-raising. Prior to any attempt to raise funds for the campaign, rules, regulations and policies relating to this activity should be scrutinized and adhered to.

MODERN CAMPAIGN TOOLS

Without going into much detail, an effective campaigner, along with his/her team, realizes that all resources at the candidate's disposal should be exploited for maximum results. These tools include marketing material, publicity/the media, campaign software to remain organized and create a database, as well as making the most use of the internet such as a website, blogs, e-mail and other sites that will add exposure and interaction with the constituents.

CANVASSING: BRINGING THE MESSAGE DOOR-TO-DOOR WHILST SELLING ONESELF

A staple of local elections in particular, door-to-door campaigning is a great way to meet people and to introduce one's candidacy. Demonstrating willingness to hear voters out, canvassing is a very effective and proven method of ensuring success on Election Day. It is most effective when utilized by small groups and doesn't have to be considered a chore but rather a fun and social event. Asking influential and supportive residents to tag along will be beneficial given that they will be construed as an endorsement of the candidate. If no one is home, a door hanger or postcard should be left with a "Sorry I Missed

You" message along with a reminder of the election date. Either way, the candidate's mark should be left behind.

DEALING WITH THE MEDIA: PREPARATION ELIMINATES THE ELEMENT OF SURPRISE

There is usually adequate media coverage during municipal elections. It may be that reporters will want to conduct an interview at least once during the campaign. A candidate should not get intimidated by reporters but instead get accustomed to them. Naturally, though, they need information from the candidate to produce their stories as much as the candidate should embrace media coverage to project his/her image and inform voters about his/her platform. It is a mutually beneficial relationship. That said, one must be careful about what is said to reporters and, as far as possible, ascertain what will be asked in advance of agreeing to an interview. Answering reporters' questions with short and concise answers is a useful strategy that helps one to avoid having his/her words misconstrued or taken out of context. Role playing in advance with someone who will ask impromptu type yet anticipated questions is a great idea — provided that speaking notes and draft responses to such questions are prepared in advance. Public speaking skills should be practiced — speaking simply, factually and in an articulate manner.

Seeking endorsements is imperative with the aim of exploiting political capital. But just as effective, are the endorsements of currently elected officials, plus the local chamber of commerce. Gaining this public backing will maintain the candidate's campaign on track and show the voters that important, politically involved people trust his/her motives.

If an aspiring elected official wants to run a political campaign, applying these strategies can increase the likelihood of success. Whether running for a local school board position, mayor or for higher office, there are certain tactics that will help, regardless of the context of the race. Exploiting all means at one's disposal offers the best chance at competing in the tough yet ultimately rewarding world of politics.

BIBLIOGRAPHY

Aaker, David A. Strategic Market Management. Hoboken, NJ: John Wiley & Sons, 1998, 2009 & 2011

Arnell, Peter. Shift: How to Reinvent Your Business, Your Career, and Your Personal Brand. New York: Crown Publishing, 2010

Burke, Ronald J. and Tomlinson, Edward C. Crime and Corruption in Organizations (Psychological and Behavioral Aspects of Risk). London: Gower, 2010

Calvin, Robert J. Sales Management Demystified. New York: McGraw-Hill, 2007

Chevalier, Michel and Mazzalovo, Gerald. Luxury Brand Management: A World of Privilege. Hoboken, NJ: John Wiley & Sons, 2008

Cusick, William J. All Customers Are Irrational: Understanding What They Think, What They Feel, and What Keeps Them Coming Back. New York: AMACOM, 2009

Davis, Richard. The Intangibles of Leadership: The 10 Qualities of Superior Executive Performance. Toronto: John Wiley & Sons Canada, 2010

Drucker, Peter F. Innovation and Entrepreneurship. New York: Harper & Row, 1985

Drucker, Peter F. The Effective Executive: The Definitive Guide to Getting the Right Things Done. New York: Harper Business, 2006

Erling, Dan. Match: A Systematic, Sane Process for Hiring the Right Person Every Time. Hoboken, NJ: John Wiley & Sons, 2011

Friedmann, Susan A. Riches in Niches: How to Make It Big in a Small Market. Franklin Lakes, NJ: The Career Press, 2007

Gerzema, John and D'Antonio, Michael. <u>Spend Shift: How the Post-Crisis Values Revolution Is Changing the Way We Buy, Sell, and Live</u>. San Francisco, CA: Jossey-Bass, 2011

Gobé, Marc. <u>Emotional Branding: The New Paradigm for Connecting Brands to People</u>. New York: Allworth Pres, 2009

Godin, Seth. <u>All Marketers Are Liars</u>. New York, Portfolio Hardcover, 2009

Godin, Seth. <u>Permission Marketing: Turning Strangers Into Friends And Friends Into Customers</u>. New York: Simon & Schuster, 1999

Goldsmith, Marshal and Carter, Louis and The Best Practices Institute. <u>Best Practices in Talent Management: How the World's Leading Corporations Manage, Develop, and Retain Top Talent</u>. San Francisco, CA: Pfeiffer, 2010

Goodman, John A. <u>Strategic Customer Service: Managing the Customer Experience to Increase Positive Word of Mouth, Build Loyalty, and Maximize Profits</u>. New York: AMACOM, 2009

Hair, Joseph F., Anderson, Ralph E., Mehta, Rajiv and Babin, Barry J. <u>Sales Management: Building Customer Relationships and Partnerships</u>. Boston, MA: Houghton Mifflin Company, 2009

Hindle, Tim. <u>Guide to Management Ideas and Gurus (The Economist)</u>. London: Profile Books/The Economist Magazine, 2008

Hope, Jeremy, Bunce, Peter and Röösli, Franz. <u>The Leader's Dilemma: How to Build an Empowered and Adaptive Organization Without Losing Control</u>. San Francisco, CA: Jossey-Bass, 2011

Kapferer, Jean-Noel and Bastien, Vincent. <u>The Luxury Strategy: Break the Rules of Marketing to Build Luxury Brands</u>. London & Philadephia: Kogan Page, 2009

Kim, Chan W. and Mauborgne, Renee. <u>Blue Ocean Strategy: How to Create Uncontested Market Space and Make Competition Irrelevant</u>. Boston: HBS Publishing Corporation, 2005

Kotler, Philip and Keller, Kevin Lane. <u>Marketing Management</u>. Boston: Pearson Learning Solutions, 2007

Lenderman, Max. <u>Experience the Message: How Experiential Marketing Is Changing the Brand World</u>. New York: Avalon Publishing Group, 2006

Lockwood, Thomas. Design Thinking: Integrating Innovation, Customer Experience, and Brand Value. New York: Allworth Pres, 2009

McNamara, Michael. The Political Campaign Desk Reference: A Guide for Campaign Managers and Candidates Running for Elected Office. Parker, CO: Outskirts Press, 2008

Michman, Ronald D. and Mazze, Edward M. The Affluent Consumer: Marketing and Selling the Luxury Lifestyle. Westport, CT, Praeger Publishers, 2006

Michonski, David M. Power Marketing for Luxury Real Estate. New York: The Stonesong Press, 2011

Mintzberg, Henry. Mintzberg on Management. New York: The Free Press, 2007

Okonkwo, Uche. Luxury Online: Styles, Systems, Strategies. London: Palgrave Macmillan, 2010

Peters, Thomas J. The Little Big Things: 163 Ways to Pursue EXCELLENCE. New York: Harper Business, 2010

Pinson, Linda and Jinnett, Jerry. Steps to Small Business Start-up. New York: Kaplan Publishing, 2006

Porter, Michael E. Competitive Strategy: Techniques for Analyzing Industries and Competitors. New York: The Free Press, 1998

Reid, Robert D. and Bojanic, David C. Hospitality Marketing Management. Hoboken, NJ: John Wiley & Sons, 2010

Ries, Al and Ries, Laura. The 22 Immutable Laws of Branding. New York: Harper Business, 2002

Ries, Al and Ries, Laura. The Fall of Advertising and the Rise of PR. New York: Harper Business, 2004

Robin Lent, Perrin, Genevieve and Tour, Alain-Dominique. Selling Luxury: Connect with Affluent Customers, Create Unique Experiences Through Impeccable Service, and Close the Sale. Hoboken, NJ: John Wiley & Sons, 2009

Spielman, Gina L. The Blueprint for a Successful Practice: Methods of Marketing Your Business & Increasing Your Bottom Line. U.S.A.: (Self-published), 2009

Wheeler, Alina. <u>Designing Brand Identity: An Essential Guide for the Whole Branding Team</u>. Hoboken, NJ: John Wiley & Sons, 2009

Ziglar, Zig. <u>Selling 101: What Every Successful Sales Professional Needs to Know</u>. Nashville, TN: Thomas Nelson Inc, 2003

www.ingramcontent.com/pod-product-compliance
Lightning Source LLC
Chambersburg PA
CBHW020424220526
45464CB00002B/553